ULYSSES & JULIA GRANT'S MISSOURI *Love Story*

VICKI BERGER ERWIN AND JAMES W. ERWIN

Published by The History Press
An imprint of Arcadia Publishing
Charleston, SC
www.historypress.com

First published 2025

Front cover, top: Julia Dent Grant and President Ulysses S. Grant. *Library of Congress*; *bottom*: White Haven before the Civil War. *National Park Service*.
Back cover: Julia, daughter Nellie, her father, Colonel Frederick Dent, son Jesse, 1865. *Library of Congress*.

Manufactured in the United States

ISBN 9781467157360
Hardcover ISBN 9781540299994

Library of Congress Control Number: 2025943125

CONTENTS

PREFACE

This book is not a biography of Ulysses S. Grant or an analysis of his military campaigns. There are many other books for those interested in that aspect of his life. Nor is it a biography of Julia Dent Grant. There are books about her, although far fewer than those about Ulysses.

We are interested primarily in their relationship, which began and flowered in Missouri in the 1840s and 1850s. It happened at Julia's family farm, White Haven, where they met and where two of their children were born. The amount of time they spent together at White Haven was a minimal but important part of their lives together. We also cover aspects of their lives before and after Missouri and how their life "in the West" affected them.

Except for the few letters Ulysses wrote, most of what we know about him during the White Haven period is based on recollections collected years after he became world-famous as a general and president. Ulysses, for example, barely mentions his civilian life in Missouri in his *Personal Memoirs*. The accuracy of others' reminiscences is often doubtful, and we had to choose those that seemed most interesting, enlightening and hopefully accurate. Most of what we know about Julia's life comes from her *Memoirs*, which scholars have acknowledged are occasionally inaccurate. And so, to the best of our ability, we have constructed a Missouri story centered on two people who loved each other very much through the hard times and the good times. We used quotations as they appear in the original works, misspellings, wrong punctuation and all.

Preface

We were inspired to write this book when we visited Hardscrabble, the cabin Ulysses Grant built, now located at Grant's Farm. We were allowed to go inside the cabin thanks to Mike Standley and his boss, employees of Grant's Farm. Its two rooms on the first floor are much larger and more comfortable than its rough exterior might suggest. And given that we regularly walk our dog around the Ulysses S. Grant National Historic Site—the location of the main house at White Haven—it seemed a natural subject for us to write about. We live on land once owned by Dent, then Grant.

We would like to thank Mike and the administration at Grant's Farm for the wonderful tour. We also wish to thank Nicholas Sacco of the National Park Service at White Haven for generously sharing his time, expertise and a flash drive full of documents that helped us immensely. Thanks also to Andy Hahn at the Campbell House for information about Grant's relationship with Robert Campbell, and Dennis Northcott and Ami Null of the Missouri History Museum for help with Grant photos. Needless to say, any errors are ours alone.

1

ULYSSES BEFORE JULIA

There was nothing about the seventeen-year-old standing before the adjutant at the U.S. Military Academy at West Point that gave any hint that he would be that entering class's most distinguished soldier. He was thin, even spindly, standing only five feet, one inch tall and weighing 117 pounds. He wore the rough clothes of a Westerner—acceptable in his home state but out of place in the home of some of his more aristocratic Southern fellow students.

He reported as "Ulysses H. Grant, from Ohio." The adjutant checked the lists of approved applicants. There was no "Ulysses H. Grant," but there was a "Ulysses S. Grant, from Ohio." Grant protested. He was told that he must go through the appointment process again if he wanted to be accepted as Ulysses H. Grant. Grant, showing his practical side, acquiesced to his new name. After all, he said, "An initial more or less does not matter."

One of the upperclassmen, William T. Sherman, remembered looking over the list of the new cadets, paying particular attention to who had been appointed from his home state of Ohio. He was amused to see that one was a "U.S. Grant." The older cadets immediately dubbed him "United States Grant" and "Uncle Sam" Grant, soon shortened to just "Sam Grant." Twenty-three years later, this man would be Sherman's commanding officer and his initials transformed by the press and public into "Unconditional Surrender" Grant.

A Young Horseman

Jesse Root Grant was what we would call today a "self-made man." His mother died when he was eleven; he and his brothers and sisters were farmed out to other families as his father simply could not make it alone and died poor. Jesse landed with Judge George Tod and his wife, Sallie, in Youngstown, Ohio. Sallie took a liking to him and taught Jesse to read and write. When he asked her what he should do with his life, she said, "If you want to get rich, you had better learn the tanning business, for all tanners get rich."

Jesse wanted to get rich.

Staring off as an apprentice, Jesse worked for his half brother Peter's tannery in Maysville, Kentucky. Later, he returned to Hudson, Ohio (southeast of Cleveland), claiming that he was glad to be rid of living in a state that permitted slavery. Jesse worked for Owen Brown, a successful cattle breeder and tanner in Hudson. He became acquainted with Owen's son John—yes, *that* John Brown. Jesse later said John was a man of "high moral and physical courage, but a fanatic and extremist in whatever he advocated," an apt description of the person who would become famous (or infamous) for the Pottawatomie Massacre in Bleeding Kansas and the Harper's Ferry Raid, both of which helped spark the Civil War.

After two years, Jesse left Brown to become a tannery foreman in Point Pleasant, Ohio. There, he met and married Hannah Simpson in 1821. At first, Jesse and Hannah lived in a modest home in Point Pleasant. On April 27, 1822, Hannah gave birth to their first child, a chunky boy weighing ten and three-quarter pounds, whom they named Hiram Ulysses Grant. Shortly after, the Grants moved to Georgetown, Ohio, about thirty-five miles southeast of Cincinnati. They had five more children: Simpson, Clara, Virginia, Orvis and Mary. As he grew his family, Jesse grew as a businessman and entrepreneur, owning multiple tanneries and stores.

Jesse Root Grant, Ulysses Grant's father. *Library of Congress.*

Ulysses Grant's birthplace, Point Pleasant, Ohio. *From James Grant Wilson, ed.,* The Presidents of the United States, 1789–1914 *(1914).*

By 1850, Jesse was said to be worth $150,000 (about $6 million today). Jesse achieved his goal.

Little is known about Hannah. She seemed to have been a quiet, even-tempered and kindly woman, living in the shadow of her more dynamic, even bombastic husband. Jesse was opinionated and ready to engage in debates. When writing for a local newspaper, he was known as "The Castigator." He was active in local politics, serving as mayor of Georgetown in 1837. Hannah kept the home and raised the children. She was described as unusually bright and very religious. One relative said she claimed no one was entitled to praise. Rather, "you ought to praise the Lord for giving you the opportunity to do it."

While his mother was devout, Ulysses was not. He attended church, but more as a duty than a desire. Perhaps it was partly due to his inability to appreciate the music at the services. He suffered from amusia, a neurological condition that makes a person unable to distinguish musical notes. One author compared it to the inability to tell the difference between Beethoven's Fifth Symphony and "Yakety Sax." In later years, Ulysses hated military music and would quote the old chestnut, "I know of only two tunes: one of them is Yankee Doodle, and the other isn't."

Ulysses's parents gave him free range about the home. From an early age, he was fascinated by horses. As young as three or four years old, he played around and under horses, unafraid of being trampled. "Horses seem to understand Ulysses," his mother said. Jesse allowed five-year-old Ulysses to take the workhorses down to the creek for water, standing on their backs as he held the reins. By age ten, he was taking passengers on a wagon forty miles and back by himself.

Hannah Simpson Grant, Ulysses Grant's mother. *National Park Service.*

In his *Memoirs*, Ulysses told a story that made him the butt of jokes around Georgetown when he was only eight. He spotted a colt owned by a neighbor, Richard Ralston, that he very much wanted. Jesse offered Ralston twenty dollars for it, but Ralston refused. Later, Ulysses begged his father to buy the horse. Jesse relented but said the horse was worth only twenty dollars. Jesse told his son

> *to offer that price; if it was not accepted I was to offer twenty-two and a half, and if that would not get him, to give the twenty-five. I at once mounted a horse and went for the colt. When I got to Mr. Ralston's house I said to him: "Papa says I may offer you twenty dollars for the colt, but if you won't take that, I am to offer twenty-two and a half, and if you won't take that, to give you twenty-five." It would not take a Connecticut man to guess the price finally agreed upon.*

Jesse was self-taught and, as his son wrote, "a constant reader up to the date of his death." He was particularly concerned that his children receive an education. Ohio, however, had no system of public education at that time. Parents resorted to subscription schools for their children, paying a few dollars to hire a teacher for three months. Ulysses attended two such schools in Georgetown. One (now known as the Grant Schoolhouse) was built in 1824. After four and a half years there, he attended the Dutch Hill School. He learned reading, writing and arithmetic (just as the old song goes). He complained later of never being taught anything about algebra until he was at West Point, except for a book he bought in Cincinnati on the trip there, "but having no teacher it was Greek to me."

Ulysses attended the Maysville Academy in Maysville, Kentucky, in 1836–37. Before going to West Point, he attended the Presbyterian

Academy in Ripley, Ohio. But he learned little new. Ulysses joked in his *Personal Memoirs* that his teachers went over the same thing that his Georgetown ones had done so often—"A noun is the name of a thing… until I had come to believe it."

Jesse may have hoped that his eldest son would take over the family business, but Ulysses had no interest in doing so. He hated working in the tannery. Instead, Ulysses preferred taking care of the family vegetable garden, training horses and providing transportation to those needing passage to other towns. Short of workers one day, Jesse recalled that he asked Ulysses to work in the tannery using a knife to scrape the flesh and hair off the hides after soaking them in the lime vat. Ulysses agreed to the unpleasant task but said,

> *"Father, this tanning is not the kind of work I like. I'll work at it though, if you wish me to, until I am one-and-twenty; but you may depend upon it, I'll never work a day at it after that." I said to him: "No, I don't want you to work at it now, if you don't like it, and mean to stick to it. I want you to work at whatever you like and intend to follow. Now what do you think you would like?" He replied that he would like to be a farmer, a down-the-river trader, or get an education.*

Jesse had no farm to give Ulysses, and he disapproved of him being a river trader. So he determined to get his son a good education. How to provide an excellent education at little to no cost? There was only one answer—West Point Military Academy. Ulysses would receive a fine college education that would open all sorts of possibilities. He didn't have to make the military a career—indeed, many cadets resigned shortly after graduating to take lucrative civilian jobs as engineers, teachers or businessmen.

One did not (and does not) just apply to West Point. Jesse needed a congressman to nominate his son, which was a problem. The congressman who held that power was Thomas L. Hamer. Jesse and Hamer were fast friends fifteen years earlier but had a falling out over politics in 1833 and hadn't spoken to each other in years. But now Tom Hamer was his only hope for his son. Jesse wrote to Congressman Hamer, asking his former friend, "If you have no other person in view for the appointment, and feel willing to consent to the appointment of Ulysses," to so indicate to the War Department. Hamer's term was about to expire when he received the letter. He hurriedly nominated "Ulysses S. Grant" (assuming his middle name was Simpson). Hamer wrote back to Jesse, "I received your letter and have asked for the appointment of your son, which doubtless will be made. Why didn't you apply to me sooner?" The fractured friendship was repaired. Ulysses would be going to West Point. All that remained was to tell him.

Ulysses was not anxious to go, and the appointment (he said later) came as a surprise to him. His father said:

> *"Ulysses, I believe you are going to receive the appointment." "What appointment?" I inquired. "To West Point; I have applied for it." "But I won't go," I said. He said he thought I would,* and I thought so too, if he did. *I really had no objection to going to West Point, except that I had a very exalted idea of the acquirements necessary to get through. I did not believe I possessed them, and could not bear the idea of failing.*

An Unpromising Cadet

Before leaving for West Point, Ulysses's uncle and cousin helped him put his initials on his trunk with large brass tacks. He contemplated it for a moment—"H.U.G."—Hiram Ulysses Grant. That would not do. It would be asking to be a laughingstock upon arrival. And so, practical as always, Ulysses decided to switch his first and middle names to a more sober set of initials (without telling his parents). He could not anticipate that further developments would saddle him with initials his fellow cadets found nearly, but not quite, as humorous as those he avoided.

In May 1839, Ulysses arrived at West Point. "A more unpromising boy never entered the Military Academy," William Sherman later wrote. Nevertheless, he easily passed the entrance exams. He was still thinking of some sort of civilian occupation. "A military life had no charms for me," he wrote in his *Personal Memoirs*, "and I had not the faintest idea of staying in the army even if I should be graduated, which I did not expect." Cadets spent the summer in basic training; they were up at five o'clock in the morning, marching and drilling and learning the craft of a soldier until ten o'clock at night. At last, classes began on August 28, and they moved from their tents to the barracks. Although Ulysses continued to sign his name as "Ulysses H. Grant" until he graduated, he settled down as Sam Grant.

Shortly after formal classes began, Sam wrote to his cousin McKinstry Griffith, praising West Point as "the most beautiful place I have ever seen."

Now that all the cadets were in uniform, Sam did not have to be self-conscious about his dress, although he did joke about what they now had to wear:

> *If I were to come home now with my uniform on, the way you would laugh at my appearance would be curious. My pants sit as tight to my skin as the bark to a tree and if I do not walk* military, *that is if I bend over quickly or run, they are very apt to crack with a report as loud as a pistol. My coat must always be buttoned up tight to the chin. it is made of sheeps grey cloth all covered with big round buttens. it makes me look very singular. If you were to see me at a distance, the first question you would ask would be, "is that a Fish or an animal?"*

Unlike his most famous opponent, Robert E. Lee, Sam did not spend four years at West Point without incurring demerits. His record in that respect was about average. In later years, he still complained of reductions in class rank because of "bad marks" assessed during the school year for petty violations of dress or etiquette or for being late to class or church. He remarked that a cadet soon learned, "Any special excellence in study would be affected by the manner in which he tied his shoes."

By his admission, Sam was not an especially diligent student. Surprisingly, he showed a knack for mathematics. Unfortunately, his French was below par. This was a problem because the school relied on French texts for instruction in military science—a reliance that continued until the Civil War.

Sam was often more interested in the novels he checked out of the school library than the works he was supposed to study. He was particularly fond of novels by Sir Walter Scott and James Fenimore Cooper. Another favorite was Edward Bulwer-Lytton, all of whose books then in print he devoured, no doubt some by candlelight on a dark and stormy night.

Sam also showed talent as an artist in Professor Robert W. Weir's class. Cadets sketched topographical maps and anatomical drawings during his second year. In his third year, Sam painted Native Americans, cityscapes and at least one instance of a draft horse. (Nine of his paintings and sketches survive at West Point.) He was quite skilled as an artist, but it was not a hobby he pursued in later life.

Ulysses was a quiet student, much as he had been back home. He was not one of the pranksters found in any large group of young men. That is not to say he was never involved in hijinks, albeit involuntarily. On the

West Point. *Library of Congress.*

way to engineering class one day, Frank Gardiner showed his fellow cadets a large heirloom watch. Ulysses held it just before they entered the room, and he quickly stuffed it inside his coat. The instructor called on him to present a problem at the blackboard. As Ulysses explained his work to the class, the watch suddenly began to go off with a sound like a Chinese gong. The instructor looked in vain for the cause of the noise while Ulysses, unperturbed, continued talking over it. The cadets had to wait for the class to be over to burst into laughter.

Although Sam was a mediocre scholar (except in mathematics), there was one subject in which he was far superior to his fellow cadets: horsemanship. The courses began in Sam's second year. Immediately, he was recognized as one of the best horsemen in class, if not the whole school. He could tame the wildest horse (as he had done at home).

The demonstration of his skill climaxed at the graduation exercises in 1843. That June, all the cadets were required to perform riding exercises before the faculty and guests, including jumping their mounts over a bar. At the conclusion of the class's presentation, the riding master raised the bar higher than a man's head. "Cadet Grant!" his voice boomed throughout the riding hall. Sam appeared astride York, a horse one of his classmates told him "will kill you some day." "Well," he replied, "I can't die but once."

James B. Fry described the scene: "A clean-faced, slender young fellow, weighing about one hundred and twenty pounds, dashed from the ranks on a powerfully built chestnut-sorrel horse and galloped down the opposite side of the hall." The rider urged the horse forward at a full gallop toward the bar and, "as if man and beast had been welded together," cleared it to "thunderous applause."

Jefferson Barracks during the Civil War. *Wisconsin Valley Library Service.*

With that satisfying ending to his West Point career, Sam Grant graduated twenty-first out of thirty-nine. Graduates were allowed to request the branch to which they wanted to be assigned. The top students were eligible and usually chose the engineers. The next most prestigious were the artillery and the dragoons (the only mounted troops in the army—there were no cavalry regiments until 1855). The latter was Grant's first choice; his second was the infantry. Given his modest academic standing, it came as no surprise that he was assigned to the Fourth Infantry Regiment as a brevet or temporary second lieutenant. (New graduates were given brevet rank until a permanent position opened.) In September 1843, Sam Grant reported to his regiment's station at Jefferson Barracks, just south of St. Louis.

While at West Point, Sam became close friends with many cadets who later served as Confederate generals, including James Longstreet. His most significant friend was his roommate in his final year—a young man from St. Louis named Frederick Dent Jr. When Dent found out that Sam's first duty station was Jefferson Barracks, he invited him to visit his family at White Haven, their farm located a few miles from the post. It came to be a place he would visit often.

2

JULIA BEFORE ULYSSES

Julia Boggs Dent's birth on January 26, 1826, in St. Louis, Missouri, was a welcome change of pace for her parents, Frederick and Ellen Dent. They finally had a daughter after four sons. She immediately became a favorite of her father and the brothers.

Julia's father, "Colonel" Frederick Dent, was born and raised on a plantation in Maryland, worked by enslaved people. (Although he served in the War of 1812, Dent's rank of colonel was only an honorific affected by many Southern gentlemen.) He was one of five children and had one half brother from his mother's first marriage. His father, George, was surveyor of what would become Cumberland County, Maryland. Frederick had no formal education. He left Maryland as an apprentice to a surveyor building the road from Cumberland to Wheeling, West Virginia. In 1802, Frederick moved to Pittsburgh, Pennsylvania, soon after his father's death. In one of his first tasks in his new job as a trader, he was sent to Spanish Louisiana and visited Missouri. For the next fifteen years, he grew a successful trade between Pittsburgh and St. Louis. He met Ellen Bray Wrenshall in Pittsburgh.

Ellen was born in England, where her father was an itinerant preacher. He moved his family to Pittsburgh to escape religious intolerance. As an ordained Methodist minister, he helped establish that religion in the city. She grew up in a wealthy, strict family and had a sheltered childhood. In her *Memoir*, Julia describes her grandfather as being very strict and that he considered it a sin "to enjoy yourself in any way."

On a Raft to a New Life in Missouri

Frederick and Ellen married on December 22, 1814. Their first child, John Cromwell, was born on May 22, 1816, in Pittsburgh. The Dents, including young John, traveled to St. Louis in 1817. Their mode of travel was unique—three log rafts chained together, each with a small frame cabin built in the middle of the raft. Frederick, Ellen, baby John and a friend, Edward Tracy, who later was associated with Colonel Dent's firm, traveled on one raft. One raft was for cooking and floated along with the third carrying servants, furniture and other goods. They disembarked from the rafts and traveled by carriage over the Illinois prairie to their destination.

Frederick's half brother had moved to St. Louis two years earlier, and he probably eased their transition from the East. In 1817, St. Louis was a bustling commercial center with American settlers sprinkled among the descendants of the original Spanish and French Creole residents. The Dents quickly found a place in St. Louis society. In 1819, Frederick founded the Episcopal Church in the city along with his business partners, Thomas Riddick and Wilson Price Hunt.

Frederick worked as a merchant at Dent and Riddick. (Julia recalls he worked in a firm with Peter Lindell, but there are no records of him

MRS. DENT, MOTHER OF MRS. U. S. GRANT.

COLONEL DENT, FATHER OF MRS. U. S. GRANT.

Ellen Wrenshall Dent and Frederick T. Dent Sr. *National Park Service.*

working for that company.) Their second son, George, was born on January 30, 1819. The Dents had a third son, Frederick Tracy Dent, born on December 17, 1820, also in St. Louis. The fourth and final son, Louis, was born on March 3, 1823. There were also four Dent daughters. Julia was the first, followed by Ellen (Nellie), born June 28, 1828; Mary, January 30, 1835 (who died in infancy); and Emily (Emma), June 6, 1836.

Little is known about Ellen Dent's life. She was educated in the East and felt she lacked many of the skills of a "western pioneer" wife. She loved to read and listen to music and shared this with her children. Julia described her mother as "handsome." Emma said she was "a small, slender woman with rather serious gray eyes, a smiling mouth, and a gentle voice." Ellen trained her household staff well and then stepped back and let them do their jobs. Mrs. Dent made sure her home was a welcoming space, a tradition Julia continued with her homes. That warm welcome and the always open door initially drew Ulysses Grant as a visitor. In the words of historian Kimberly Scott Little, the Dent home had a "mix of pioneer spirit, old Southern charm, and Eastern gentility."

White Haven: A History

White Haven—the farm on which Julia was raised and where she and Ulysses lived for most of their time together in Missouri—was first partially cleared and cultivated by Native Americans. In 1796, the Spanish government granted Hugh Graham 800 arpents (about 681 acres) of prime farmland on Gravois Creek. It had ample water, with the creek and a spring that fed into a tributary of the Gravois. There was good soil and extensive woods. Graham did not own it for long. In 1799, he sold it to James MacKay, a well-known explorer, adventurer and fur trader. MacKay explored western Canada and the Dakotas long before Lewis and Clark. When they were preparing for their voyage, he provided them with a valuable map to aid their exploration of the Louisiana Purchase.

MacKay married Isabella Long, the daughter of John and Elizabeth Long, a prominent family in early St. Louis. In 1808, James and Isabella gave William Lindsay and Elizabeth Sappington Long a portion of the property as a wedding present. Lindsay (he went by his middle name) and Elizabeth probably lived in a log cabin on the property.

Painting of White Haven before the Civil War. *National Park Service.*

Between 1812 and 1814, Lindsay and Elizabeth began constructing what was and is the main house on the farm, using several enslaved persons. Despite St. Louis's French heritage, the main house was built with a timbered frame with horizontal clapboards characteristic of New England homes, rather than the French "palisade" design with upright posts set in in the ground. It had upstairs and downstairs porches (Julia called them "piazzas") on the front of the house. Its one French attribute was its roof, which was not centered and covered the house and the porches without a break, necessitating having its twin fireplaces and chimneys offset to the rear rather than centered on the roof.

The original house had two spacious rooms on the first floor. Each had a front entry door opening on the porch and was connected by a hallway running from the front of the house to the back door. The upstairs also had two rooms reached by stairs in the hallway. There was a third-floor attic.

The Longs did not finish the house. Indeed, when they sold it to Theodore and Ann Lucas Hunt in 1818, it still had a dirt floor. The Hunts finished the house's interior and added two rooms on the rear. In 1820, Frederick Dent began assembling the White Haven estate by purchasing the main house and land surrounding it from the Hunts for $6,000. By 1840, Frederick owned several parcels of land on each side of Gravois

Creek, stretching from what is now Rock Hill Road to Eddie and Park, bounded by Pardee Road on the north and Gravois Road on the south—a total of 862.7 acres. He added a parlor on the south side of the house by moving an existing cabin (built with vertical logs in the French style) in the 1830s, and he replaced the two front doors with windows and built a single door that opened on to the hall. Dent also added a stone summer kitchen and slave quarters immediately behind the house, as well as a chicken house and an icehouse on the spring that fed into a small creek. At one time, there were perhaps as many as a dozen cabins across the creek from the main house where the enslaved persons he owned lived.

Frederick named the farm White Haven after his ancestral plantation in Maryland.

Life on the Farm

Enslaved people (eventually totaling thirty) did the housework and farmwork at White Haven. Dent operated in the manner of a gentleman. According to Hamlin Garland, he "commanded labor, but did not act with it." He spent the summer reading the news and arguing with neighbors on the front "piazza" and the winter doing the same in a warm corner of the house by the fireplace.

Dent was, however, a progressive farmer. He had the first thresher in the neighborhood and one of the first reapers. He raised horses, cattle, hogs and imported fowl. He had a second business trading real estate and was among those in the area known as "land rich, cash poor." The vagaries of the economic situation often placed Dent in a precarious financial situation.

The Colonel dressed in black and always wore a black hat after discarding his white ones. When asked why he had changed his preference, Dent replied only gamblers wore white hats, and anyone, on seeing one, would immediately think that man was a "black leg." Julia overheard this conversation, and as a child, when she saw a man wearing a white hat, she looked for his black legs.

On the other hand, Ellen didn't like White Haven as much, feeling that a move to the country separated her from the friends and connections she had made in the city. However, it was Frederick's choice, and she made the best of it.

The Dents had friends far and wide, including the socially prominent men and families of St. Louis. They claimed friendship with both Governors William Clark and Alexander McNair.

Julia's four brothers—John, George, Fred and Louis—attended St. Charles College, where their uncle, John Fielding, was the president when it opened. John was the only one not to finish. Fred, of course, attended West Point as well. They (like Julia would later) brought home fellow students who made Julia a pet and let her go riding, hunting and fishing with them. Louis, the brother closest in age to her, was also the brother who was her closest companion. They explored fields together, and he often read to Julia.

John was the wild child of the group, playing truant from school as often as he could and spending his college years as a prankster. After one incident, John was placed "inbounds," meaning he was confined to the campus. The area's young women put together a petition to have him released because, they claimed, the community's social life could not continue without John's presence. Fred was what their mother termed a "huntsman," who loved the outdoors and hunting and was somewhat of a "dandy," dressing the part of a hunter.

Fred and Louis formed the Gravois Hunting Club with neighbors' sons. The club excluded the German neighbors, and a feud, whether over this or some other slight, arose between the Dent sons and the sons of John and William Sigerson. One evening, the Sigersons' haystacks and outbuildings burned. A rumor arose that the Dent boys started it. One of the Dent sons (which one is unknown because it was originally reported as Frederick, who was away in the army—John is the likely suspect) engaged in a fight with the Sigersons and almost died from head injuries. After leaving college, John floated between working in the city and working at White Haven, hoping his father would leave the main property and house to him.

A Rosy Childhood

Julia's memoir paints a rosy picture of her childhood at White Haven. Her brothers were heroes to her, and her sister and the enslaved children on the plantation were her playmates. She had the run of the surrounding landscape, accompanied (as she later wrote) by "a dusky train of from eight to ten little colored girls of all hues" and chaperoned by an African American nurse.

They fished, rode horses, hunted wild strawberries and built playhouses for their fairy friends along the brook. Having their children play with enslaved children close to them in age was common for slaveholders and performed a dual purpose. Playmates were always available, and it gave the white girls a chance to "practice" being owners of the enslaved and molded the kind of mistresses they would be as adults. Julia did not question her role as mistress to the enslaved.

Throughout her life, Julia attended church and ensured her children and Ulysses did, too. Church meetings provided much of her social life in the country. One of the preacher's messages about faith made an impression on Julia. He told the congregation that even a small amount of faith would allow the believer to move mountains and walk on water. Julia had the opportunity to put what she'd learned about faith into practice soon after.

She and her sister Nell were gathering flowers along Gravois Creek and wanted to include a certain flower that grew on the far side of the water. Heavy rain had swollen the creek, and their usual crossing was under water. How could they cross? Julia remembered her preacher's message and told her sister they could cross on faith. When Nell asked what that meant, Julia replied, "Believe that you can, and you can."

Julia was certain it was a matter of walking across the water and was surprised when, after her first steps, she found herself drenched up to her armpits. Nevertheless, she continued to the other side. Nell started across and met the same fate, except she panicked in the middle of the creek instead of continuing. Julie rescued her sister, and they ended up sitting on the bank in wet clothes, waiting until their garments dried and the creek water receded enough to cross back.

The Dent children attended Gravois School, and it was a positive experience for Julia. Her brothers sometimes carried her to school in a "chair" made by clasping their hands together. Sometimes, her nurse carried her; sometimes, she rode a small pony led by one of the enslaved; sometimes, she rode behind her brother Louis. Julia was popular with the older girls who wanted to get to know her brothers better. Julia mentions no teasing or negative comments about her eyes. She was born with a condition known as strabismus or crossed eyes. Either the children she socialized with were uncommonly kind, or Julia didn't want to dwell on anything negative, a trait she carried with her throughout life.

The schoolhouse was built of logs, about twenty-five feet square. The teacher's desk was located to the right of the one door to the building on the east wall. A fireplace filled the north wall. Girls sat near a long, narrow window on the west side, and the boys (big boys in the back and smaller in front) sat near high, wide windows on the south side. There were no backs on the seats, so Julia's mother had a special armchair made for her daughter's comfort.

The school sported a grass playground, worn in spots by the students playing games. The girls played jump rope, "open the gate as high as the sky and let King George and his men pass by" and Ring Around the Rosie, among others. According to Julia, a favorite activity was telling and listening to fairy tales.

A brook passed through the schoolyard, and a spring gushed over a rock at the bottom of a hill on the opposite side of the brook. The children drank from the spring.

Julia learned what she wanted to learn, and her teachers, for whatever reason, tolerated her choices. John Fenton Long taught at the school in 1836. His father was the original owner and builder of White Haven. John Long later became a neighbor of the Dents and a friend of Grant. But first, he was Julia's teacher. One weekend, he assigned the class to learn Roman numerals and told them he would punish them if they didn't do so. Long called on his own sister first, and she hadn't learned the lesson. He punished her with a rod. Julia was called on next and whispered to her teacher that she thought she knew them when she came into school but didn't know them now. Long forgave her lapse and said, "You will learn it in good time." Julia never did.

When Julia was almost eleven years old, her parents enrolled her in the Misses Mauros's Academy for Young Ladies, a boarding school in St. Louis City at Market and Fifth Streets. She remained there until the age of seventeen.

As indicated by her performance at Gravois School, Julia wasn't a superlative student. She maintained a course of studying only what she liked. When teachers tried to discipline her for her refusal to stay within the curriculum, Julia refused to recite English grammar or learn math. She excelled when she was engaged in a subject she liked, such as philosophy, mythology or history. Julia enjoyed reading, not particularly what was assigned but current popular fiction. After she read *The Dashing Lieutenant*, she stated her future husband would be "emphatically a soldier, a gallant, brave, dashing soldier."

Julia returned home to White Haven on alternate weekends, always bringing a teacher or friends with her to enjoy her family's hospitality. The family enjoyed these weekend visits and visitors as much as Julia did and were proud to show off their farm.

After almost seven years of finishing, Julia left Misses Mauros's School in June 1843—at the same time Ulysses and his roommate, Julia's brother Fred, graduated from West Point.

3

"GRANT WENT A-COURTIN"

Julia spent the summer of 1843 at home. Her society during that time consisted mostly of socializing with friends and families from Jefferson Barracks, as it was closer to White Haven than the city. In September, Julia moved back to St. Louis, staying with the O'Fallon family, Colonel John, his wife (a cousin of Colonel Dent) and their daughter, Carrie (Caroline), a great friend of Julia's. Mrs. O'Fallon became a society mentor to the young woman.

Julia attended her friends' weddings and debutante balls, entertained by the young men of St. Louis and the young officers of Jefferson Barracks.

The Handsome Lieutenant

On his initial visit to White Haven, the first member of the Dent family Ulysses encountered was young Emma, not yet seven years old. She was in the fields with four enslaved playmates, collecting birds' nests. Emma's arms were full of nests when Ulysses rode up and asked if Mr. Dent lived there.

In "'When Grant Went A-Courtin,'" Emma writes that she was embarrassed and could only stare at him without saying a word. She knew from his uniform he was a soldier from the Barracks and thought him "the handsomest person I had ever seen in my life." When he asked again if Dent lived there, Emma finally answered, "Yes, sir," and dropped the birds' nests and a tiny bird she'd been holding.

Brevet Second Lieutenant Ulysses Grant's 1843 graduation portrait. Julia's sister Emma proclaimed him to be "pretty as a doll." *National Park Service.*

Emma and the coterie of playmates followed the lieutenant to the house, where he introduced himself to Colonel Dent, Mrs. Dent and Nellie and explained that his classmate at West Point, Fred, had invited him to visit his family. The Dents welcomed him. Mrs. Dent sent Emma off to play, but Ulysses so enchanted her she remained sitting on the steps, staring at the handsome visitor.

Years later, Emma claimed she knew Ulysses best because she met him first and knew him longest (obviously forgetting that Fred had been his roommate at West Point well before Grant showed up at White Haven).

Emma described Ulysses's good looks, concluding he was "pretty as a doll." He was "youthful looking, even for his age.... His cheeks were round and plump and rosy; his hair light. His features were regular, pleasingly molded, and attractive, and his figure so slender, well-formed, and graceful that it was like that of a young prince to my eye." Seeing him in this way, sitting on an equally handsome horse, it is no wonder Lieutenant Ulysses Grant was Emma's first crush.

Fifteen-year-old Nellie, the young lady of the house in Julia's absence, also enjoyed Ulysses's company. And he was a frequent visitor, riding to White Haven several times a week to spend the afternoon and sometimes staying for supper.

Then Julia came home. Ulysses said, "My visits became more frequent; they certainly did become more enjoyable."

Ulysses and Julia took to one another from the beginning, which was unusual for them. In fact, in later years Ulysses admitted that it was a case of love at first sight for him.

At that time, Julia was small and dainty but could not be described as a beauty. As mentioned, she suffered from strabismus, or crossed eyes, where the eyes point in different directions. But Julia had an "exquisite figure." Her best features were her small, slender hands and feet and her thick, chestnut hair. She had brown eyes, a rosy complexion and a positive outlook that she carried with her through life.

In addition to the younger sisters and older brother Fred, Julia's mother was a fan of Ulysses from the beginning. When Ulysses first showed up at White Haven, he was not well. He stood five feet, eight inches tall, weighed 117 pounds and had a persistent cough. This aroused Ellen's motherly instincts, and she took it upon herself to feed and medicate him. She was impressed with his humble demeanor and the common sense he displayed in arguments with Colonel Dent, who was not impressed. Ellen said of the young soldier, "That young man will be heard from some day. He has a good deal in him. He will make his mark."

Julia and Ulysses loved to ride, explore nature in the nearby woods and grounds on their walks, fish and discuss the books they'd read. Julia liked to work with the flowers at White Haven, and Ulysses shared her love of growing things. Julia's brothers and sisters often joined them, but sometimes, they would slip away from the crowd, leaving young Emma in such a foul mood that Ulysses had to coax her out of it upon their return. After all, Emma knew him first and best, according to her.

One of the couple's favorite occupations was riding. Julia had a Kentucky mare named Missouri Belle, and the horse was fleet of foot. Ulysses had brought his horse from Ohio, and it was equally fine-blooded. The two of them often raced in the early morning or after dinner.

Julia and Ulysses also participated in the neighborhood's social activities, picnics, dances and camp meetings. Julia was a good dancer, but Ulysses, although he would accompany her, would not dance. On one occasion, they attended a camp meeting with their friends. The group traveled in a farm wagon furnished with chairs and hay. After the last hymn was sung, they started home, and a thunderstorm came up. No homes were nearby, and the frequent lightning made sheltering under the trees dangerous. A tarpaulin happened to be in the wagon, but there was no way to secure it as a covering. One of the soldiers, Robert Hazlitt, later to become a casualty of the Mexican War, was the tallest of the men and became the center pole with the tarp hung over him to protect the girls from the worst of the storm. The men, however, were soaked.

In the spring, after the two had met, Ulysses secured a twenty-one-day pass to visit his parents in Ohio. When he came to tell Julia and the Dents goodbye, he managed to meet Julia alone on the piazza. He offered his West Point class ring to her, and she knew this "gift" was meant as an engagement ring. She gently refused, citing her mother's displeasure if she accepted it. Julia considered Ulysses her good friend, joining the ranks of other friends among the officers at Jefferson Barracks.

While he was traveling, the Fourth Infantry was ordered to Louisiana. When he arrived home, Ulysses received a letter from a friend from the regiment, telling him not to open any official correspondence until his leave was up. Ulysses knew what that meant—he was to leave Missouri. "I now discovered that I was exceedingly anxious to get back to Jefferson Barracks," he later said, "and I understood the reason without explanation from any one."

While Ulysses was visiting his family, Julia missed him more than she'd imagined she would. Lieutenant Hazlitt told Julia that if Grant didn't return within a week, he was already headed to Louisiana. At the end of that week, Julia rode out to Jefferson Barracks and waited, hoping for his return. When Ulysses didn't appear, she returned home, saddened, realizing perhaps her feelings for Ulysses were more than friendship.

Unfinished Business

Both Julia and Ulysses were superstitious. Julia believed in "premonitions, omens, and the foretelling of the future in dreams." These omens and foretelling were seldom ominous, and she simply looked at them as confirming the decisions she'd made or the actions she'd taken were the right ones.

Julia received one of her foretellings while Ulysses was in Ohio. She superstitiously believed that dreams the first night in a new bed would come true. And Julia had a new bed. A tradition was to name each bedpost for a potential or wished-for husband. She labeled one for Ulysses. If one of the men appeared in the dream, he would be the husband. Julia dreamed that Ulysses arrived at White Haven dressed in civilian clothes. When he sat down beside her, she asked him how long he would stay. He replied he was there for a week. When she recounted the dream to her friends and family, they scoffed at the possibility it would come true. After all, Ulysses was on his way down the Mississippi River and headed for Louisiana.

However, Ulysses could not head into war without clarifying things with Julia. When he returned to Jefferson Barracks and found his unit sent away, he asked for a few more days.

There had been a series of heavy rains, swelling creeks around the Barracks and White Haven, including the Gravois, which Ulysses had to cross to reach Julia. One of Ulysses's superstitions was "when I started to go anywhere, or to do anything, not to turn back, or stop until the thing intended was accomplished." He rode his horse into the churning water and nearly drowned, ending up swimming across beside the horse. Because his uniform was completely soaked, he stopped at Julia's brother John's home and borrowed dry clothing.

Julia was about to retire for an afternoon rest when her maid announced the arrival of Lieutenant Grant—wearing civilian clothes (that were oversized on him). She quickly freshened up and joined him in the parlor, asking how long he intended to stay. His answer? He would try to stay a week, exactly as foretold in her dream.

During that visit, Ulysses obtained permission to drive Julia—just the two of them—to a friend's wedding. He used the time to declare his love for her and ask her to marry him. Julia responded that she was yet too young to be married but would like to be engaged. And so they were. Secretly. Julia recalled she wasn't ready to tell her father, and Ulysses was "too shy to ask father." Still, Julia accepted his West Point class ring and gave him one with her name engraved on it.

Julia told her sisters about the engagement, and they knew that once Julia decided to marry Ulysses, she would marry Ulysses. In Colonel Dent's own words, he was unable to deny his favorite child anything.

> *Julia was our first daughter and a delight to me. Spirited and outgoing I let her have her way in almost everything. "Would little daughter like to do this?" "No!" Then little daughter did not have to do it. She was a good little girl and not the least spoiled by my indulgence.*

After agreeing to the engagement, Julia went so far as to start a quilt for her hope chest, a quilt she never finished yet carried with her wherever she went. Julia never was one for needlework, partly because of her poor eyesight. The quilt became a symbol to her family of her tendency to procrastinate.

4
SEPARATION

Life was more exciting for twenty-two-year-old Ulysses Grant. He had just become engaged to the fascinating love of his life, eighteen-year-old Julia Dent, and was now on a steamboat heading south to New Orleans to join his regiment in his first deployment from garrison duty. Political tensions were high as Congress debated whether to annex Texas.

Camp Salubrity

The Fourth Infantry had moved to Camp Salubrity, a few miles from Natchitoches, in northwest Louisiana. On arriving at his new post on June 3, 1842, Ulysses was bursting with news. He wrote Julia the next day "with the most pleasing recollections of the short leave of absence which prevented my accompanying my Regiment; and as well, with the consequences of the leave." He joked that he explored New Orleans—"a tolerably large place"—in one day fast enough to see nothing and stopping long enough to learn nothing. But if he couldn't be stationed at Jefferson Barracks, he would be happy to be in New Orleans.

The trip to Natchitoches and Camp Salubrity on the Red River was less than pleasant. The boat was crowded with riverboat gamblers and other unsavory passengers. The camp, located on a high ridge away from the unhealthy river bottom, was plagued with clouds of insects and small lizards who "were so very intimate and sociable on a short acquaintance as to visit our tents, [and] crawl into our beds."

The chatty letter concluded with his regret at having to leave, a request to write soon and a puzzling series of twenty-three blank lines that Ulysses said would express his feelings more than words. (When Julia finally responded to the letter, she confessed that she had no idea what the blanks meant.)

Lieutenants U.S. Grant and Alexander Hays at Camp Salubrity, Louisiana, with their horses Dandy and Sunshine. *Library of Congress.*

Ulysses also sent a letter back home to an old friend from Ohio, Mrs. George H. Bailey. His eagerness to tell someone of his engagement to Julia was obvious: "My trip to this place…was marked with no incident, Save one, worth relating and that one is *laughable curious, important, surprising &c. &c.* but I cant tell it now. It is for present a secret, but I will tell it to you some time. You must not guess what it is for you will go wrong." Most likely, Mrs. Bailey could tell from the giddiness of Ulysses's letter precisely what had happened—the young man had met a girl.

The soldiers of the Fourth Infantry settled into their routine at Camp Salubrity. Recruits filled the company rosters, but several officers were detailed to serve on a staff that needed expanding to handle potential war duties. Ulysses's dream of being sent to teach mathematics at West Point died—the Fourth Infantry could not spare him. The officers socialized, played cards and trained the new men. They were part of an "Army of Observation," ostensibly in Louisiana to prevent raiders into Texas but actually (as Grant and others knew) as an implicit threat to Mexico if it decided to oppose the proposed annexation by the United States.

Six weeks passed—more than two months after the secret engagement—and there were no letters from Julia. "Be punctual in writing to me," he wrote, and "I will be compensated in a slight degree,—nothing could fully compensate—for your absence." Ulysses thought of her constantly. He wondered if her mother knew their secret. Her brother Fred half suspected. If Fred found out somehow, Ulysses wouldn't mind, but he would not tell him. He certainly did not speak to any of his fellow officers at Camp Salubrity of the engagement. "Julia," he pleaded, "write to me soon and give a long account of how you pass your time." Ulysses worried that Julia's parents would disapprove of him sending her letters that were not in response to hers—apparently a violation of nineteenth-century etiquette. He had assumed it was acceptable because Julia told them that both Ulysses and his friend and fellow officer, Robert Hazlitt, sent her letters without objection from her father or mother. Although he had not yet received a letter from his love, he "carefully preserved the lock of hair you gave me." At least one of his letters to Julia was sent in a package to the wife of Lieutenant Theodoric H. Porter, one of his fellow Fourth Infantry officers, presumably to be delivered to her without her parents' knowledge.

A Delightful Time in the City

Julia remembered that the days while Ulysses was at White Haven on leave were particularly beautiful and pleasant. Yet they were tinged with anxiety about the looming war in Mexico. What *was* Julia doing that summer after he left? She may have been engaged to a handsome young lieutenant, but she was only eighteen years old. That was no reason to refrain from having fun by attending parties and dances at Jefferson Barracks or in St. Louis. After all, the engagement was secret. If only to keep up appearances, she would continue the lively social life young women enjoyed. And of course, her eye condition made writing difficult. She probably told herself that when Ulysses's letters arrived, she *would* write to him as soon as—well, as soon as possible.

Julia and her sister were enjoying the society of 1840s St. Louis. Nell was home from school and was bored with life at White Haven in the winter. She persuaded their father to allow them to spend the season in the city. There, eligible young men serenaded them at midnight outside their window. Nell teased the "half-dozen nice, handsome, manly young fellows pouring out their very souls in song" by throwing a glove or flowers. Serenades happened so often that the neighbors complained, although the girls insisted there was nothing they could do. Julia says in her *Memoirs* that it was Nell who flirted, and one has to wonder whether she did not take part in the fun herself despite her pending engagement. The ruckus caused by the serenades finally reached a point where the neighbors warned them to tone it down, or they would report them to their father, who would take them back to White Haven. Even there, the two women entertained gentlemen callers for high tea on Sundays, much to their mother's dismay at such a practice by good Methodists on the Sabbath. Julia said it was Nell who especially sought and enjoyed male company.

Julia also developed an interest in phrenology, hypnotism, mind reading, second sight and premonitions. This interest continued throughout her life.

Julia was preparing to become a wife during this time as well. She obtained a hope chest and began to learn how to handle a household from her mother. These were more lessons that did not grab her interest, and Julia didn't bother to explore fully. And why would she? She'd been cared for by enslaved servants her entire life. Her father had granted her four enslaved people, and they would be available to perform the household duties she wasn't interested in doing.

At last, two letters from Julia arrived on August 31, addressed to Lieutenant Porter. (One of the letters had been mistakenly opened by Porter. Porter suggested that she put a cross on the envelope next time so he would know it was for Ulysses and not for him.) Julia revealed that Mrs. Dent did not think the engagement "serious." The young woman couldn't keep her secret from her mother for long. Her happy social life may have made her mother believe the engagement wasn't genuine. And if her mother knew, would she have revealed it to her father? Perhaps it would be best to have things in the open. At least, they could send each other letters directly rather than through third parties as they had done up to this point.

Ulysses mused, "I think in the course of a few days Julia I will write to Col. Dent to obtain his consent to our correspondence; I will ask nothing more at present but when I get back to St. Louis I will lay the whole subject before him." Julia asked him to go ahead and ask her parents straight out for permission to write her directly. After mulling the idea over for a week, Ulysses decided that he should ask Mr. Dent's consent to allow their correspondence. He seemed uneasy with the deception they had engaged in so far. "I have long thought it a duty to write." But it was not an easy task.

> *You can scarcely concieve the embarrassment I felt in writing such a letter, even in commencing the first line. You must not laugh at it Julia for you have the chance. I send it unsealed that you may read it before delivering it....I immagined all the time that I saw your Pa & Ma reading it and when they were done raising all kinds of objections. Youth and length of acquaintance*

> *I feared might be brought against us but assure them my dear Julia that the longest acquaintance, or a few years more experience in the world could not create a feeling deeper or more durable.*

As winter approached, the Fourth Infantry constructed huts to replace the tents (Ulysses called them "linen mansions") they were living in. With a number of officers detached, Ulysses (still a brevet second lieutenant) was left as the only officer in the company and took over as its temporary commander. The months dragged on, and he heard nothing from Colonel Dent about the request for permission to correspond openly with Julia. After the new year, Ulysses concluded that he could write to Julia "as a friend" and send the letters to her at the Sappington post office instead of surreptitiously addressed to someone at Jefferson Barracks. After all, "if not very strong in favor of my request," it was reasonable to conclude that the absence of a response could mean they had no objection.

A CONDITIONAL ENGAGEMENT

During Ulysses's absence, Colonel Dent had some financial reverses. He had borrowed money secured by a mortgage on White Haven to make ends meet. He pressured Julia to consider some of the wealthy suitors serenading under her window. Feeling torn between her father and her fiancé, Julia offered to let Ulysses out of the engagement. He, of course, said he would entertain no such thing.

At last, Ulysses had another chance to see Julia when he received a brief leave in April 1845. This time, he was determined, as he said in his August 1844 letter, "to lay the whole subject before him," meaning Colonel Dent.

It was a Sunday afternoon. The house at White Haven was filled with neighbors and friends to wish Colonel Dent goodbye and safe travels because he was leaving the next day for a trip to Maryland and Washington to settle a land dispute. As the group was enjoying drinks and conversation, who should ride up but Lieutenant Grant on a borrowed dappled gray horse! Ulysses was no longer the pink doll of sister Emma's description. Julia was struck by his now bronzed and hardened looks. He greeted the company and discreetly touched Julia's hand, but no more than that.

After greeting Julia and the neighbors on the porch, he entered the parlor where Ellen and the Colonel sat. Ellen, sensing why Ulysses was there, left the men alone. Emma, eavesdropping outside, recounted the following exchange.

> *"Mr. Dent," Ulysses said, "I want to marry your daughter, Miss Julia."*
> *My father looked back at him and smiled. (I was peeping through the shutters.)*
> *For a minute the older man did not answer but sat soberly thinking. The soldier boy awaited his answer, unmoved.*
> *"Mr. Grant," my father spoke at last. "If it were Nelly you wanted, now, I'd say 'Yea.'"*
> *"But I don't want Nelly," said the soldier, bluntly. "I want Julia."*
> *"Oh, you do, do you?—Well, then, I s'pose it'll have to be Julia."*

In a different version, the Colonel was supposed to have said that while Julia's sister Nell might be suited to being a soldier's wife, Julia was not. If that were the problem, Ulysses replied, he would resign his commission and become a teacher. His objection countered, Dent said he thought it best that Grant remain in the army. He gave them permission to correspond, and as Julia later told it, he reluctantly agreed: "If we who were so young should not change our minds in a year or two, he would make no objection." The Colonel would think it over and write with a definitive response. That was enough. The engagement was sealed and approved, if only conditionally.

Ulysses and Julia spent a blissful ten days together at White Haven, reading, walking and riding. The weather was beautiful, and the flowers were blooming. She recalled that they sat on the piazza surrounded by "one bower of eglantine and white jessamine. I remember how pleasantly the hum of the bees in that bower of ours and how near the swallows would come as they whirled past us, making music with the fluttering of their wings." But soon, Ulysses had to return to his regiment. She would not see him again for three years.

5
COMBAT

At Camp Salubrity, Ulysses anxiously awaited word from Julia and her father again. Neither wrote for weeks. In the meantime, it became apparent that the annexation of Texas would go forward and that some troops at the camp—possibly all of them—would soon be sent to the new state.

By early July, the Fourth Infantry was in New Orleans. Julia sent him a letter, but Mr. Dent did not. Ulysses was in suspense, waiting for Dent's full consent to their marriage, and he was concerned that he would be too far out of touch to receive an answer for some time. Just before the regiment's departure for Texas, a visitor from St. Louis—Mrs. Higgins, the wife of a fellow officer, brought some bad news. She told him that he had a rival for Julia's hand and that she would no longer write to him. He didn't believe it. Surely, if it were true, she would have told him herself and not sent such a devastating message by a third party. Ulysses begged Julia to write soon and reassure him that all was well between them.

The Agonizing Wait for a Response

Suffering from this internal turmoil, Ulysses sailed with his regiment for Corpus Christi, at the mouth of the Nueces River, to become an "Army of Occupation." Tensions between the United States and Mexico remained high. Although Texas was incorporated into the Union, its southern boundary was fuzzy. The Americans who settled Texas had no one living south of the Nueces River. Indeed, few persons from anywhere lived between the Nueces River and the Rio Grande River, some 150 miles away. Both the United States and Mexico claimed the land. The army sat on the edge of the disputed territory, waiting to see if Mexico would take some action that would justify war.

While the waiting game dragged out, Ulysses received a letter from Julia affirming that she still loved him and chastising *him* for not writing often enough. Given that she was the one who was tardy in answering letters, he replied tactfully they need not wait to receive a letter before responding to it and promised to write to her every two or three weeks. At the end of September, Ulysses was promoted to full second lieutenant.

Ulysses was nevertheless contemplating leaving the army. He and Julia had been engaged for a year and a half. He thought it was time to consider seriously getting married and their future together. "I have always expressed myself willing you know my Dear Julia to resign my appointment in the army for the sake of overcomeing the objections of your parents, and I would still do so; at the same time I think they mistake an army life very much." The head of Hillsboro College in Ohio offered him a professorship in mathematics. (Ulysses said the school's principal asked Jesse Grant to write his son, but one wonders whether it was the other way around.) Ulysses wrote back asking for details and said he would seriously consider the matter. He had until the spring of 1846 to reply. Ulysses's family back in Ohio repeatedly suggested that he accept the offer. Perhaps the prospect of their son going into combat sparked their urgency.

Ulysses, however, would decline the offer unless Julia wanted him to take it: "No one now can have more influence than just yourself. Tell me plainly what you think of resigning for a place of the kind." He added, perhaps to placate the old man, "If you can muster courage mention the matter to your Pa." Ulysses much preferred the army, and ultimately, he did not take the opportunity to teach.

Nonetheless, he pressured Julia to speak to her father about their marriage. The exasperation with the delay in getting a response from her father came through in a January 2 letter:

> *Here it is now 1846 Julia, nearly two years since we were first engaged and still a time when or about when our marriage is to be consumated has never been talked of. Dont you think it is now time we should press your*

father further for his concent? If you would speak to him on the subject I think he would give his concent; you know he told me that you never spoke to him of our engagement and in fact would hardly give him a chance to speak to you of it. If you think it best I will write again to him.

You know Julia what I think we would be justifiable in doing if his concent is still witheld and I hope you think nearly with me. Wont you give the matter a serious concideration and tell me soon, very soon if we agree. You alone Julia have it in your power to decide whether in spite of evrything we carry our engagement into effect. You have only to decide for me to act. If you will set a tim when I must be in Missouri I will be there no matter if my Reg't is still in Texas. The matter is one of importance enough to procure a leave of absence, and besides for the love I bear my dear Julia I would not value my commission to highly to resign it. I ought not to commit this to paper where there is danger that it may be seen before you get it, but I cannot help it, it is what I feel and have expressed before. My happiness would be complete if a return mail should bring me a letter seting the time-not far distant-when I might "clasp that little hand and call it mine."

Ulysses was happy to learn that Julia did not want him to leave the army, "although all the letters I get from my father are filled with persuasion for me to resign." He only mentioned the possibility of leaving if that was the stumbling block to their marriage.

Oddly, Julia still did not speak to her father about gaining his consent to the marriage, even though he had known about the engagement for months. The lack of news on this front was a frequent complaint in Ulysses's letters, along with pleas for Julia to write more often. Sometimes, when mail calls were disappointingly bare, Ulysses would pull out all of the letters he had received since he left Missouri and re-read them.

"Bullets Have Less Horror When Among Them Than in Anticipation"

Having failed to provoke a reaction from the Mexican government by their camp in Corpus Christi, U.S. authorities decided it was time for the army to move into the disputed area. In March 1846, the Fourth Infantry and other troops under General Zachary Taylor started a monthlong march to the banks of the Rio Grande near Matamoros. They built a small fort on the river. A couple of months later, General Taylor took the bulk of his army—about 2,500 men—to Point Isabel, the nearest port, to obtain supplies. While they were gone, the Mexican army attacked the garrison left behind across from Matamoros. Taylor gathered his forces for a return to lift the siege. The war the Polk administration sought had begun. It was a conflict Ulysses regarded as unjust and one about which he expressed some regret in later years that he did not have the moral courage to resign in protest. But he was a U.S. Army officer, trained for this job. At the time, he believed he had no choice but to follow orders and do his best in combat or whatever the future might hold for him in Mexico.

On May 7, 1846, Taylor led his small army out of Point Isabel. Ulysses was apprehensive; he wrote in his *Personal Memoirs* that some men eagerly anticipate battle, but "the number of such men is small." Others pretend to seek combat but take a different view when it first appears. He fell into the second category. He was proud to be in the army, but when he saw the Mexicans lined up against them, he began to regret having enlisted.

The next day, they finally encountered the Mexican army, drawn up in a battle line in front of a band of tall trees—*palo alto* in Spanish and thus the name given to the ensuing battle. U.S. forces were also in line of battle. Some three thousand of them, including artillery, were in a field of stiff, needle-like grass reaching their shoulders. Taylor paused to have details secure water from a nearby stream and then began to advance.

The American artillery, firing shell and canister, cut swaths of dead and injured men through the Mexican line that were quickly closed up. "There is no great sport in having bullets flying about one in evry direction," he wrote Julia, "but I find they have less horror when among them than in anticipation."

The Mexican artillery fired solid shot. The soldiers could see the cannon balls ricocheting through the tall grass like deadly bowling balls and easily dodged them. As they drew closer, however, the artillery fire became more lethal. One whizzed near Ulysses. It took off an enlisted man's head and broke up his musket, with the pieces of the weapon injuring a couple of other men. The ball continued and hit Captain John Page, ripping off his lower jaw. Miraculously, he survived, with his tongue hanging down below his windpipe, only to die a few days afterward. (This first encounter with the horror of war so impressed itself on Ulysses's mind that he not only wrote about it in explicit detail to Julia and a friend of his a few days later but also recounted it in his *Personal Memoirs* forty years later. One wonders how the sheltered twenty-year-old daughter of a Missouri gentleman farmer received

Battle of Resaca de la Palma, May 9, 1846. *Kelloggs & Thayer, Library of Congress.*

the graphic description of Page's wounding and whether it increased her concern for her fiancé's safety.)

The next day, Taylor's little army caught up with the retreating Mexicans at Resaca de Palma. It was a confusing fight in the underbrush that fragmented the battle into individual firefights. The Mexicans, thoroughly defeated, scrambled across the Rio Grande. Ulysses downplayed his role there. His company commander was sent on a scouting party to feel out the Mexican position, leaving Ulysses in command. He led the company to the right of the U.S. line. The entire battlefield was in a chaparral so dense that no one could see more than five feet. They came under fire from an unseen enemy. He ordered his men to lie down—"an order that did not have to be enforced." As the enemy began to pull away, he saw a small band of them in front. Ulysses led his men in a charge and captured a few stragglers and a wounded Mexican colonel. In his *Personal Memoirs*, Ulysses sardonically recalled that the "ground had been charged before. My exploit was equal to that of the soldier who boasted that he cut off the leg of one of the enemy. When asked why he did not cut off his head, he replied, 'Some one had done that before.'"

Taylor's little army then occupied Matamoros across the Rio Grande. They stayed there for several months. Ulysses's anxiety about whether Julia's parents agreed to their marriage filled every letter he wrote. He worried—do they speak of the engagement? Do they say yes or no? Julia, you never tell me what they say!

The other members of Julia's family had no doubts, however. Her brother Fred started calling Ulysses his "brevet brother." (A brevet was an honorary rank that did not confer the privileges or authority of a permanent rank.) Emma Dent thought the whole episode's secrecy and the hesitancy to seek Dent's consent was a farce. "After all, it was nonsense for father to be pretending that he had anything to say about it. Julia, having once said Yes, had made the decision for him. When Julia wanted a thing from my father, she always got what she wanted."

In September 1846, Taylor was on the move again. This time, his army would have a tougher nut to crack—the fortified city of Monterrey. In a bloody three-day battle, the American army seized most of the town. Realizing that further assaults on the enemy in a restricted urban area would entail even more casualties than the five hundred already suffered, he agreed to let the Mexican army withdraw. Ulysses, who was named regimental quartermaster the month before over his objections, could not remain behind with the supply trains. On his own, he rode to the sound of battle. He wrote in his *Personal Memoirs* that he lacked the moral courage to return to his post, but he wanted to be part of his company's attack on the city.

The regiment's adjutant, Lieutenant Hoskins, lost his horse. Ulysses gave him the one he was riding, but then Hoskins was almost immediately killed. Colonel Garland told Ulysses to take over Hoskins's duties temporarily. In a post-battle letter to Julia, Ulysses said, "I passed through some severe fireing but as yet have escaped unhurt." It was a bit more than that. As recounted in his *Personal Memoirs*, Ulysses rode to the rear to have more ammunition sent forward. In doing so, he had to pass across side streets filled with Mexican soldiers who shot at anyone who appeared. Ulysses threw one leg around the cantle of his saddle and hung on the side opposite the enemy, Indian-style, as he rode through the streets of Monterrey.

Ulysses found the camps after the battle strangely silent and lonely. So many men had fallen, including his good friend Robert Hazlitt. But cheerful rumors spread among the soldiers that the war would soon be over. Ulysses hoped it was true because "fighting is no longer a pleasure," he wrote to Julia. Plus, it would allow him to return to the Gravois farm and marry her—a sentiment he expressed continually during the years they were apart. To console himself, Ulysses wrote in an October letter,

> *I then took up a Journal that I kept whilst at Jefferson Barrack* [the journal has never been found] *and read as far as to where I had mentioned "that of late I could read but very little for I was so busy riding about and occasionally visiting my friends in the country—who by the way are becoming very interesting." That part Julia must have been written about the time I first found that I loved you so much. It brought the whole matter to mind and made me think how pleasantly my time passed then.*

Diplomatic efforts to end the war failed. He had to endure another winter in what was beginning to seem like an endless war. However, the Fourth Infantry would continue the fight elsewhere in Mexico under a new leader. It left Monterrey and returned to Texas. There, after a few weeks, they boarded ships to become part of General Winfield Scott's expedition to Vera Cruz.

Ulysses returned to duties as regimental quartermaster and commissary. While others maneuvered and attacked the town, he disgustedly reported to Julia that during the siege, he "had little to do except to see to having the Pork and Beans rolled about." Scott's army began its move into the interior of the country.

It was confronted by a force of more than five thousand men at a rocky mountain pass known as Cerro Gordo. Once again, Ulysses was a spectator. Led by an intrepid engineering officer—Captain Robert E. Lee—American troops wound their way around the enemy's flank and attacked them from the rear. The Mexican army was routed and fled the battlefield so precipitately that Ulysses reported that they captured the elaborate carriage of General Santa Anna (who lost a leg in 1838), complete with one of his cork legs and $30,000 in gold. After the battle, Ulysses wrote:

> *It was war pyrotechnics of the most serious and brilliant character. While it was a most inspiring sight, it was a painful one to me. I stood there watching the brigade slowly climbing those ragged heights, each minute nearer and nearer the works of the enemy with our missiles flying over their heads, while white puffs of smoke spitefully flashed out in rapid succession along the enemy's line and I knew that every discharge sent death into our ranks. As our men finally swept over and into the works, my heart was sad at the fate that held me from sharing in that brave and brilliant assault. But our batteries did their duty, and no doubt helped in achieving the glorious result.*

Ulysses tried to resign as quartermaster and resume his duties as a line officer with his company. His commander, Colonel Garland, refused, writing that this was a job from which he could not resign, regardless of how valuable his service with the company might be. The request was bucked up all the way to the War Department without success. Ulysses defiantly said: "I *must* and *will* accompany my regiment in battle, and I am amenable to court-martial should any loss occur to the public property in my charge by reason of my absence while in action."

After the victory at Cerro Gordo, there was yet another hiatus before Scott's army advanced on Mexico City. Some four thousand volunteers' enlistment expired, and he had to wait four months for replacements. Ulysses was at a low ebb, waiting for more action. He wrote to Julia, regretting that he had not taken his father's advice and resigned his commission. He would no doubt be comfortably in business had he done so. Ulysses lamented that he had not accepted the offer of the professorship in Ohio. He dreamed that he was on recruiting service in Missouri near White Haven. He was lonely, homesick, tired of war and had been denied the opportunity to be in battle with his fellow soldiers.

When Scott finally resumed his march on Mexico City, he decided to attack from the south and west. (Ulysses wrote to someone, whom the editor of his *Papers* says is unknown, that he thought the attack could have been made from the northwest and avoided all of the obstacles—forts, ditches and morasses—that hindered the army's efforts. But he admitted that he was a mere lieutenant and not privy to General Scott's information.) Once again, the intrepid Captain Robert E. Lee reconnoitered and led American troops through difficult terrain south of the city.

Ulysses repeated his actions at Matamoros, leaving his quartermaster duties behind to be on the front line with the Fourth Infantry. He participated in the bloody charge at Molino del Rey, which those in the battle called an "utter imbecility." Julia's brother Fred was wounded, but not seriously. Ulysses survived unscathed again.

The Fourth Infantry continued its assault on the city but halted at the San Cosme Gate. Ulysses looked for reinforcements or artillery to help force the issue, but none came. He scouted to the right of the American position, where he discovered a locked church. He pounded on the door. A frightened priest opened it. Ulysses, in his broken Spanish, "convinced" the priest to let them in. Ulysses directed his small band to wrestle a mountain howitzer to the belfry. There, they fired on the Mexicans at the San Cosme Gate.

By the end of the day, additional troops and artillery had arrived. The Mexican army defending the gate was battered severely. Ulysses's division was ready to push into the city the next day, but General Santa Anna abruptly left, and the American army captured Mexico City. The war

Grant at the Capture of the City of Mexico. *Emanuel Lewis, for* Frank Leslie's Illustrated Newspaper, *Library of Congress*

was effectively over. Ulysses received brevet promotions to first lieutenant and captain for his bravery in actions during the taking of the city.

Ulysses was ready to go home. He felt as though he had aged ten years. The tropical sun had burnished his skin to a deep brown, and he'd grown a full beard. Ulysses was tired of combat, tired of Mexico and, most of all, tired of his separation from Julia. But it was not to be. Ulysses remained in Mexico for another ten months, sightseeing much of the time. He went to a bullfight, a "sight to me sickening. I could not see how human beings could enjoy the suffering of beasts." He and some fellow officers attempted to climb Popocatepetl, the highest volcano in North America, but didn't reach the top because of severe weather. They visited the great caves of Mexico in the Cuernavaca Valley, which he compared to Mammoth Cave in Kentucky in size and beauty.

Finally, on July 16, 1848, Ulysses boarded a transport for the trip back to the United States, Missouri and Julia Dent.

6
MARRIAGE—AT LAST!

When Ulysses returned after the Mexican War, Julia had been waiting and preparing for their marriage for four long years despite her active social life while he was gone. She had her trousseau and her hope chest. There was no reason to delay the wedding any longer. Ulysses, or Dudey, as Julia called him, though still a first lieutenant, had decided to stay in the army. With an income of $1,000 per year, food for the family and forage for his horse, he could provide for them.

Caroline O'Fallon threw parties for the couple. They attended theater performances. Julia had become quite fond of the theater in the four years without Ulysses. And they sat together, holding hands, gazing into each other's eyes, and planning for their future together.

Ulysses made a quick trip to Ohio to visit his family and tell them of the wedding. The Grants refused to attend based on their strong opposition to slavery, and the Dents, of course, were a slaveholding family.

The Loveliest Wedding Gown

On August 22, 1848, Julia Dent and Ulysses Grant were married at the Dents' St. Louis home at Fourth and Cerre Streets. It is unclear why they weren't living at White Haven then. Two years earlier, Colonel Dent advertised the property for sale but hadn't found a buyer. He was likely meeting with economic reverses and rented the property to meet the loan payments due.

Dent home at Fourth and Cerre, St. Louis, where Ulysses and Julia were married on August 22, 1848. This view is from the 1930s. It is now a parking lot. *Missouri Historical Society*.

The evening of the wedding was hot, rainy and humid. Julia had planned to wear an India mull muslin dress her mother had worn at her wedding. However, her friend and mentor, Mrs. O'Fallon, arrived carrying a large white box and inside was her gift to Julia—a beautiful, rich, soft white watered silk gown and a tulle veil decorated with a wide fringe. Julia said later, "I never saw a wedding gown as lovely as mine." Another family friend brought Julia a corsage of white cape jessamine with enough left over to create a wreath for the veil. The friend disclosed she had nursed her flowers for weeks to have enough for the wedding.

Sources disagree as to the attendants at the wedding. Julia reports that her bridesmaids were her sister Nellie, Sarah Walker and her cousin Julia Boggs. The young ladies wore white. She remembered that Lieutenant Cadmus Wilcox, Bernard Pratte and Sid Smith were Grant's groomsmen, but she was wrong. Unfortunately, Sidney Smith had died in the Mexican War. James Longstreet, a future Confederate general and Ulysses's good friend from West Point, is often mentioned as the third groomsman. However, Longstreet mentioned only "attending" the wedding in his memoir.

There were a limited number of guests at the wedding as the house was small. Reverend J.H. Linn performed the ceremony, followed by cake, ices and fruit. There was music at what we would call the reception, although there was no dancing due to limited space.

As Ulysses did not have a lot of money, his wedding gift to Julia was a miniature daguerreotype of himself encased in a gold locket with a velvet ribbon that fit around Julia's wrist. This became her favorite picture of her husband and a treasured keepsake.

The couple spent the night at the family home, and the next day, Julia left St. Louis for the first time in her twenty-two years, taking her first trip on a boat. Their honeymoon was to be spent in Ohio visiting Grant's family, also a first for Julia—meeting her in-laws.

Julia found the Grants pleasant but different from her family. They were cordial but not as warm as she was used to with the Dents. She did enjoy hearing the stories of her husband's childhood. She and Ulysses visited relatives and friends throughout the countryside. Julia was pleased with her reception and her new extended family, and Ulysses was pleased Julia liked his kin.

According to some accounts, the newlyweds returned to White Haven in late summer; according to Julia, they returned in mid-October. Perhaps to her, it seemed longer than it was. Ulysses's leave was over, and his new orders sent him north to Detroit.

At this point, Julia realized she was leaving the home where she had spent her entire life and would have to go forward into a life with strangers. She sobbed at the thought as if her heart was breaking. Poor Ulysses had no idea how to respond. Julia, he knew, always looked forward to what the next day might bring, but now she was distraught. The two of them were in the parlor, and Ulysses was telling Julia he wasn't sure what to say to her reaction to them moving into their married life. He had spent four years looking forward to it, but now she seemed reluctant. Colonel Dent chose to join them at that moment. Julia recalled the following conversation:

> *My father said: "Grant, I can arrange it all for you. You join the regiment and leave Julia with us. You can get a leave of absence once or twice a year and run on here and spend a week or two with us. I always knew she could not live in the army."*

> *Ulysses' arm was around me, and he bent his head and whispered: "Would you like this Julia? Would you like to remain with your father and me go on alone?"*
>
> *"No, no, no, Ulys. I could not, would not, think of that for a moment."*
>
> *"Then," he said, "dry your tears and do not weep again. It makes me unhappy."*

They never spoke of the matter again.

A Military Wife

The Grants headed north. Another first for Julia was going forth without any of the enslaved people Colonel Dent had given her. She would be responsible for making her bed, cooking their food and all the myriad tasks involved in housekeeping. There was a danger in letting enslaved servants live in free states. Legal precedents held that an enslaved person could declare themselves free after a certain amount of time. Julia, for one, couldn't understand why her "people" would want that. Didn't they have everything they needed given to them? The ethos of growing up in a slaveholding family in a slave state was ingrained in her.

Julia was now a military wife. They were supposed to go to Detroit but ended up in Sacketts Harbor, New York, for a year before moving to Detroit. She had to make new friends wherever they went, keep house (Ulysses finally hired a girl to help) and manage a budget. Given Julia's difficulty and dislike of numbers, this task was difficult, yet she was successful. Julia led an active social life during these years and recalled the posting as pleasant in her *Memoirs*. And she became pregnant with her first child.

Julia promised her father she would return to White Haven for the child's birth. Frederick Dent Grant was born on May 30, 1850, not at White Haven, but at the Dent home in St. Louis. Julia was attended by her mother and Mary Robinson, one of the enslaved. Julia had made a layette for her new son and thought, "No one had ever had such a fine, great boy." Ulysses joined his wife and new son in June, and the family returned to Detroit before moving to Sacketts Harbor again.

Ulysses was unhappy with his work as a quartermaster. He found it boring and repetitious, nothing but a lot of paperwork. And he wasn't sure there was any future in it for him.

Military post at Sacketts Harbor, New York. *New York Public Library.*

When the move to Sacketts Harbor was announced, Julia and baby Fred set out to spend the summer at "home," White Haven. Her family wanted to see how Fred had grown. Julia spent the summer once again with help to care for the baby. In September, Ulysses wrote, telling her she needed to return because he was anxious to see his son, and Julia said, "I think he said me too."

Ulysses was supposed to meet his family in Detroit to accompany them the rest of the way to Sacketts Harbor. Julia dismissed the nurse at that point, yet her husband didn't show. Now solely responsible for caring for her child, she decided to travel alone to Buffalo, where he would surely meet them. When he didn't, Julia felt quite anxious, as well as frazzled by caring for Fred. She boarded a train to finish the journey. That night, a large man jumped out of his seat and gave a frightful cry. Julia was scared enough by the cry, but that grew to terror when she learned the man was on his way to be locked in a mental institution. She left the train at the next stop and spent a few days recovering from the incident. She finally reached her destination, grateful to be back with her husband.

Fred was the only baby at the post and, as a result, was everyone's pet. He spent time with the soldiers in the mess hall, performed feats of agility with the troops and perhaps developed his first taste for military life that winter.

Two momentous events occurred the next spring. Ulysses's regiment received orders to go to the West Coast, and Julia became pregnant with her second child. The couple discussed having Julia and Fred accompany Ulysses to his new posting but ultimately decided it would be too treacherous a journey, especially in light of the pregnancy. Ulysses took his leave on July 5, and Julia and Fred traveled to Ohio to await the birth of Ulysses S. Grant Jr. on July 22, 1852, overseen this time by Ulysses's mother, Hannah. The new son was soon nicknamed Buck because he was born in Ohio, the Buckeye State.

7

RESIGNATION AND RETURN TO MISSOURI

It was just as well that Julia and the children stayed home because Ulysses encountered disease and death crossing the Isthmus of Panama. His first post was Fort Vancouver in Oregon Territory, a beautiful but godforsaken place far from his beloved Julia. His depression was not relieved when he was assigned to Fort Humboldt near Eureka in Northern California.

Misery in the West

It is fair to say that the winter and spring of 1854 was the nadir of Ulysses Grant's life. After "a long and tedious journey," he arrived at Fort Humboldt, California, on January 4. The fort, 250 miles north of San Francisco, was just some log huts and cabins surrounded by a low earthen wall. It was located near Eureka on a bluff above Humboldt Bay, with an expansive and likely beautiful view, if you weren't suffering from intense homesickness and loneliness.

Ulysses assumed command of Company F, Fourth United States Infantry. The fort's commander was Robert Buchanan, of whom the kindliest thing that was said about him was that he was a martinet. Years before, Ulysses got on his bad side at Jefferson Barracks when he repeatedly returned to the post late in the evenings after he visited Julia at White Haven.

To make matters worse, the fort was so isolated that the mail, which Ulysses eagerly awaited, depended on whether passing ships could negotiate the difficult waters of the bay. Ulysses's letters to Julia grew progressively despairing. "You do not know how forsaken I feel here!" he wrote in February. Young Fred was growing up, and Ulysses had never seen his second son, Buck. On March 6, he wrote that he was tempted "to resign and trust to Providence" that he would be able to support the family back home. All he

needed was some assurance of employment with moderate pay, but then the specter of "*poverty, poverty*, begins to stare me in the face, and then I begin to think what would I do if you or the little ones should want for the necessaries of life."

On March 25, Ulysses complained once again that Julia had not written to him since the preceding October, or the letters had been lost (a frequent excuse he gave for her failure to write that he first used during their long

Fort Humboldt, Eureka, California, Ulysses Grant's last post on the West Coast. *Library of Congress.*

separation during the Mexican War). Don't wait for your father or brother to go to St. Louis to write a letter to be mailed—that was just an excuse. Just go to the nearby Sappington post office, he urged. The failure to hear from Julia and the desire to see his children was becoming too much. "I do not feel as if it was possible to endure this separation much longer."

Things came to a head in April 1854. At long last, Ulysses's promotion to captain came through. He acknowledged receipt of the promotion and accepted it on April 11. On the same day, he submitted his resignation from the army: "I very respectfully tender my resignation of my commission as an officer of the Army, and request that it take effect from the 31st July next."

The circumstances of his resignation remain uncertain. In his *Personal Memoirs*, Ulysses said that he resigned because he concluded that he could not support his family financially as an army officer. But, as he wrote to Julia in March, he had no plan for supporting them as a civilian.

Given the later obsession with Ulysses's drinking habits, both during the Civil War and later by his biographers, it is inevitable that stories circulated that he had been threatened with punishment for showing up drunk on duty. It is possible, maybe likely, that they were true. Army officers of the period, especially those on lonely duty at remote posts, were often known to overindulge in alcohol. There was little else to do at a place like Fort Humboldt.

Ulysses's drinking problem that supposedly led to his resignation was only reported years later (there is no contemporary evidence of it at all). However, it was claimed (again, only after he became nationally famous) that these rumors spread in the closed society of the 1850s army at the time. Nonetheless, as reported by early biographer Hamlin Garland and accepted by many later ones, the story goes as follows: It was payday at Fort Humboldt—probably April 9 (two days before his resignation). Ulysses had been drinking to excess the night before and woke up still tipsy. The army practice was for the company commander to pay his men personally. Ulysses's roommate, Lieutenant Lewis Hunt, recognized his less-than-stellar condition and offered to replace him. Ulysses refused and took his place at the table to pass out money due to his men. Colonel Buchanan saw that Ulysses was intoxicated and sent him to his quarters. Later, he demanded that Ulysses either resign or stand for a court-martial. Other officers urged Ulysses to go to trial. The punishment would hardly fit the crime, and he would likely be acquitted. Ulysses, already forlorn and aching for a return to Missouri, decided that resignation was the proper course of action.

Or so the story goes.

Ulysses fell ill in February and April. He was so sick that Major Buchanan reported on May 1 that he was still unable to leave the post. It seems likely that he had a recurrence of malaria he originally contracted in childhood that laid him low for a month. The symptoms could have been misconstrued as drunkenness, as some of his friends later explained about similar rumors that circulated in St. Louis in the 1850s.

While Ulysses was stationed in the West, Julia decided to return to White Haven. She felt the Grants disapproved of her child-rearing methods and decisions. White Haven also had room for the boys to play, not to mention household help for Julia. At "home," she once again participated in social and church activities in the neighborhood, including the wedding of her brother Fred.

Mostly, Julia was a mother to her sons, Fred and Buck. She objected to young Ulysses's nickname to no avail; she always called him by his given name. Fred was almost three years old and moved into wearing pants. Upon being granted this new big-boy privilege, he stretched as tall as possible and asked his mother, "Mamma, do you think my papa is as large as I am?" Fred was forgetting what his Papa looked like, and little Buck had yet to meet him.

Fred would not let his younger brother outdo him in any way. In one incident, little Ulysses made a circle with his arms and said to Julia, "Mamma, I love you this much." Fred quickly said, "Mamma, I love you as much as the sky out in the country."

Julia read to the boys and gave them lessons daily, mostly about everyday objects, leading to information about their world. For example, she asked them where the tall wardrobe in the house came from. They were surprised to learn it started as a tree; their clothes were once sheep coats; the window glass started as sand. She was delighted by their curiosity and questions—until those questions exceeded her knowledge.

People Julia referred to as "pretended personal acquaintances" reported that Ulysses was "dejected, low-spirited, badly dressed, and even slovenly" at his post in the West. Tales of his excessive drinking accompanied these rumors. Julia was quick to deny them. "Well, I am quite sure they did not know my Captain Grant, for he was always perfection, both in manner and person, a cheerful, self-reliant, earnest gentleman." Scholars acknowledge that Julia undertook the writing of her *Memoirs* in part to clear up any smears about the reputation of her dearly beloved husband.

In any event, Ulysses found a boat to San Francisco, where he lingered for a few days. He received his back pay and proceeded to Panama to catch a ship for New York. This is another one of those stories about Ulysses that came to be repeated later: While in Panama, he met an old soldier named Babcock, who was sick and suffering from rheumatism. Babcock wanted to go home but lacked the money for his passage. Ulysses gave him $40 to pay for it, leaving him with only $10 for the rest of his trip.

Ulysses tried to recover $1,600 owed to him by Elijah Camp, now the sutler at Sacketts Harbor. Writing from New York City, Ulysses told Camp

Julia with Fred and Buck (Ulysses Jr.). According to Nicholas Sacco, this is the first known photo of Julia, circa 1850s. (Note that Julia preferred her picture be taken from a side view. Here, she is presented full face.) *National Park Service, Ulysses S. Grant Historic Site.*

he was coming to collect the debt. This was not a good idea, for Camp had left by the time Ulysses arrived. Ulysses went back to New York City poorer than when he left. He met Simon Bolivar Buckner, a friend from West Point. Buckner paid for a hotel room for Ulysses. Jesse sent money that allowed Ulysses to repay Buckner and secure passage to Ohio.

The meeting with Jesse in Bethel was probably strained. His father was quite upset with him. Jesse had worked hard to have his son appointed to West Point. Ulysses spent eleven years in the army and served honorably in the Mexican War. Jesse had bragged about Ulysses's exploits there. He tried hard to save his son's commission.

Congressman Andrew Ellison discovered that Ulysses had resigned from the army and telegraphed the news to Jesse. Ellison requested on Jesse's behalf that Ulysses be given six months' leave instead of accepting his resignation. Secretary of War Jefferson Davis replied that the resignation had already been accepted. Jesse wrote to Davis himself:

> *If it is consistent with your powers & the good of the servis I would be gratifyed if you would reconsider & withdraw the acceptance of his resignation—and grant him a six months leave, that he may come home & see his family. I never wished him to leave the servis. I think after spending so much time to qualify himself for the Army, & spending so many years in the servis, he will be poorly qualifyed for the pursuits of privet life. He has been eleven years an officer, was in all the battles of Gen Taylor & Scott except Buenavista, never absent from his post during the Mexican war, & has never had a leave of six months—Would it then be asking too much for him, to have such a leave, that he may come home & make arangments for taking his family with him to his post. I will remark that he has not seen his family for over two years, & has a son nearly two years old he has never seen. I suppose in his great anxiety to see his family he has been induced to quit the servis—Please write me & let me know the result of this request.*

Davis replied that Ulysses gave no reason for his resignation, and in any event, it was accepted. The resignation was "therefore, complete, and cannot be reconsidered." Whether Ulysses was "poorly qualified for the pursuits of privet life" remained to be seen.

Ulysses did not record how he felt about his father's efforts to get his resignation rescinded. He certainly knew that Jesse was disappointed in his decision, the more so because he had not been consulted about such an important step as giving up his military career. Ulysses's mother was never enthusiastic about his army career and was likely happy that he had decided to become a civilian, whether he consulted her husband or not. Hamlin Garland wrote she "was glad to see him out of the service" and away from the temptations of drink and gambling for which the army was notorious.

"A Well-to-Do Missouri Farmer"

Father and son might have discussed whether Ulysses was interested in joining his brothers in the family business at one of Jesse's stores in Ohio or Illinois. But Ulysses had his mind set on going back to Missouri. He supposedly told his fellow officers before getting on the boat to San Francisco, "Whoever hears of me in ten years, will hear of a well-to-do Missouri farmer." Jesse's neighbors said that he complained that "West Point spoiled one of my boys for business," to which Ulysses replied, "I guess that's about so." He left Jesse for Julia and what would become his home for the next five years.

Ulysses's homecoming was, as one might expect, an emotional one. He arrived on August 20 in a buggy, haggard and worn from a trying time on the West Coast, an awkward reunion with his disgruntled father and an anxious trip to Missouri. Julia had no idea when he might return, so she dressed carefully every day as if that were the day she'd welcome him back. She had changed little during her husband's time in the West, but Ulysses was different. He had new lines in his face, and he looked tired. Emma recalled that one of her sister's enslaved "entourage" was the first to see him. "For Lord's sake! Here is Mr. Grant!" she called. Fred and Buck were playing on the front porch. At first, they were frightened by this strange man. Ulysses had been gone for two years. Fred may have forgotten what he looked like and was hesitant when this person picked him up and hugged him. Buck had never seen him. Julia rushed outside. The family was together at last.

Jesse Grant was disappointed and upset with his son, but we do not know what Colonel Dent thought. While Ulysses's exit from the army meant Dent's favorite daughter would not be following her military husband to some distant post, it also meant that her husband was starting over at the age of thirty-two. Even Ulysses admitted that he had to "commence…a new struggle for our support." Julia's brothers and sisters were doing much better. Nellie married a doctor, Louis (sometimes spelled Lewis) was a judge in California and Fred Jr. was a successful and decorated army officer.

In the meantime, Ulysses, Julia and the children lived in the main house at White Haven. Neighbors later claimed there was a strained atmosphere at the farm during that time. Ulysses and Dent were said to have extended discussions—one might call them arguments—about various matters, political and otherwise. And certainly, when the war came in 1861, they had far different views about the propriety of secession. But they lived together for the better part of five years before the war, and the Colonel came to live in the White House after Ulysses was elected president. Most likely, Nicholas Sacco concludes, there was mutual respect, admiration and even a bit of playfulness in their disagreements.

But in 1854, Frederick could not have been too pleased that his favorite daughter was married to a man with no prospects other than farming on land Dent had provided. Ellen Dent always liked Ulysses and no doubt welcomed having her grandchildren close by.

On the other hand, the elder Dent must have been grateful that Ulysses immediately pitched in to help on the farm, working alongside the old gentleman's enslaved farmhands. Ulysses chafed at idleness and was always looking for something to do. At age sixty-seven, Dent was happy to let Ulysses take care of the farm and harvest the crops. He cemented Ulysses's and Julia's intention to stay close by allowing them to use eighty acres of land on the north end of White Haven. (He seems to have kept title to the tract—as her father did with the enslaved persons he gave to Julia—possibly thinking he would leave that property to her on his death.)

In late September 1854, the Grants visited Ulysses's parents in Covington, Kentucky, where Jesse and Hannah had moved. The family traveled by boat, and the sun shone on them for nearly the entire journey. As they stepped ashore, the sun disappeared behind a dark cloud. "I hope this is not ominous of our visit," Julia said, another of her premonitions. Ulysses assured her it was not.

Having reconciled himself to Ulysses's decision to become a civilian, Jesse offered him a position at his store in Galena—but on condition that Julia and the children live in Covington. Ulysses declined. He much preferred a farm life to being a merchant, and no doubt the clincher was that he had just spent two miserable years away from his family. Why should he be separated from them again? Another consideration was that Julia felt less than welcome with her husband's family. Jesse disapproved of slavery—and Julia's experience in Detroit and Sacketts Harbor convinced her she could not live without the help of her enslaved servants.

Moreover, Hannah thought Julia was extravagant for having someone else do her housework "and she couldn't think well of a daughter-in-law who employed slaves, though she said very little about it." The couple returned to White Haven for the winter of 1854–55. Ulysses was determined to make the best of the situation there.

Whether the mood at the main house at White Haven was idyllic or tense that winter, in the spring of 1855, Ulysses and Julia moved to Wish-ton-wish, about three-quarters of a mile southwest of the main house. Julia's brother Louis had built Wish-ton-wish a few years before. It was a two-story brick house with stone accents—Julia described it as an "English villa." Their only daughter was born there on July 4. Ulysses wanted to name her Julia, but Julia had always hoped to name her daughter Ellen after her mother. At the christening, Ulysses gave in, and the baby was named Ellen, soon shortened to Nellie.

HARDSCRABBLE

Louis's home was comfortable, but he could return from California anytime. The main house at White Haven was also cozy and roomy. It was nice to have family nearby, but the newly reunited couple wanted their own place. And so, each day in 1855 when he did not have to work on Dent's farm, Ulysses trudged the nearly two miles from Wish-ton-wish down a steep hill to Gravois Creek and up another steep hill to the property Dent had given them. Julia chose the site for their new home. There, he cleared the land and cut and cured logs for the new house. He also found a new occupation to help pay for his family's support—woodman.

Ulysses, with the help of one or two enslaved men, cut down trees and sawed them into lots suitable for sale in St. Louis. He either borrowed a couple of enslaved men from Dent or hired others. At some point, Ulysses purchased an enslaved man named William Jones from Colonel Dent, who may have worked with Ulysses cutting trees. However, considering the price of adult male slaves in Missouri at the time and Ulysses's reduced circumstances, the purchase may have been at a nominal cost. Regardless of who helped him and how many, it was hard work. Ulysses later said, "I moistened the ground around these stumps with many a drop of sweat, but they were happy days after all." Ulysses bought two fine horses for his wagon. Each day, he and his men loaded the wagon, and he took it the ten miles to the Twelfth Street market in the city. When the wagon was full, he walked beside it into town because the horses had enough to haul without adding a "lazy rider."

He is often pictured as unkempt and slovenly during his time as a farmer. But it's been pointed out this may only be because of the contrast with his later life. He loved his wife, his children and the fact they were together. To him, that was a measure of success. One neighbor observed that "his supreme happiness centered in his home." Even though Julia had never had to live so simply before, they had, according to her sister Emma, "plenty to eat and plenty to wear and no dependence upon any relative."

Years later, as president, he liked to reminisce about his wood-hauling days. In a story he told Isaac Sturgeon, a St. Louis friend, and often repeated at White House dinners, Ulysses explained that he didn't get up at the crack of dawn to haul wood because it was too cold. He met his competition coming back from town as he was heading in:

> *The fact that their labors were over, never bothered me at all. I lost nothing and gained considerable. It was only possible to make one trip a day, so that by taking my morning nap I yet had plenty of time to reach the city, dispose of my wood and return before dark. They lost their sleep and gained nothing in the price of their wood; I gained my sleep and lost nothing in the price of the wood.*

Jefferson Barracks was still a major military post, and officers Ulysses knew at West Point and in the Mexican War passed through there. He often saw old friends while delivering wood to the market.

One day, General William S. Harney stopped a wagon on the street. The driver was dressed in rough clothes with his axe and whip beside him in the seat. Harney looked once and then more carefully.

"Why Grant, what in blazes are you doing here?"

"Well, General," Ulysses replied, "I'm hauling wood."

Harney laughed uproariously and insisted that Ulysses come to dinner with him at the Planters Hotel—the finest in St. Louis—despite his attire.

On another occasion, one of Ulysses's old friends from Mexico stopped a farmer on the road. He asked where a former soldier named Grant lived. "Well," said the man, "I am he." Shocked, the officer asked, "Great God, Grant, what are you doing?" Ulysses responded, "I am solving the problem of poverty."

The most famous reunion Ulysses had with an old army buddy was with James Longstreet. They had been fast friends at West Point, and Longstreet had attended the Grants' wedding. Longstreet was still in the army. He and other officers had gathered at the Planters Hotel for a card game. But they needed a fourth. One of the officers, a classmate of Ulysses named Edward Holloway, said he would go outside and find someone. He returned with the shabbily dressed Ulysses. They were hail fellows well met and he enjoyed the card game, although Ulysses was never much of a gambler—at cards.

Longstreet felt very unhappy because "Grant had been unfortunate, and he was really in needy circumstances." The next day, Longstreet said:

> *I was walking in front of the Planters', when I found myself face to face again with Grant who, placing in the palm of my hand a five dollar gold piece, insisted that I should take it in payment of a debt of honor over 15 years old. I peremptorily declined to take it, alleging that he was out of service and more in need of it than I.*
>
> *"You must take it," said he, "I cannot live with anything in my possession that is not mine." Seeing the determination in the man's face, and in order to save him mortification, I took the money, and shaking hands we parted.*

Ulysses and Longstreet would not meet again until April 10, 1865—the day after Lee's surrender at Appomattox

On another trip to the city, Ulysses met another old soldier—a carpenter from Ironton who came to St. Louis to repay a debt. It was Babcock, the man he met in Panama, to whom Ulysses had lent $40 to pay for his passage home. Babcock paid him the $40 plus $10 in interest. Ulysses was surprised and pleased. "I believe this is the first interest I ever received in my life, and I didn't know I was a capitalist before."

Despite the stories about Ulysses as the humble woodman, the business was hardly unprofitable. Historian Kimberley Scott Little calculated that he made a sum that compared favorably with his military salary. Plus, Ulysses showed some cagey business sense. Colonel Dent had an enslaved man, Old Bob, who he probably brought with him from Maryland, cut wood for White Haven's stove daily. Ulysses struck a deal with local miners to deliver wood for mine props at five dollars per load and a load of coal sufficient to heat the main house for the winter.

By the summer of 1856, the house Ulysses and Julia were planning for the property they received from her father was ready to assemble. Ulysses had cut the logs, shaped them with an adz, split the shingles, dug the cellar

Hardscrabble (1891) as it likely appeared when the Grants were living there. *Missouri Historical Society*.

and collected stone for the foundation and chimneys. The house raising was a big party. The neighbors, among them members of leading local families, the Longs and Sappingtons, came to help and brought some of their slaves. Food and drink were liberally distributed, and the house walls were raised in a day or two. Ulysses finished the construction by caulking the logs, installing the windows and laying the floors.

Julia planned the layout. On the first floor were two large rooms, a sitting room and a parlor, separated by a hall. Upstairs were the bedrooms. Emma said that Julia wanted "an old-fashioned house built in the old-fashioned way—log laid upon log by friendly hands," but it was probably Ulysses and the Colonel who chose to build a log cabin rather than a frame house. Biographer Lloyd Lewis said the neighbors believed Ulysses built a log cabin because that was all he could afford. The family moved into the place in October 1856.

Julia professed to love the house but admitted in her *Memoirs,* "I did not like it at all, but I did not say so."

Hardscrabble interior, 1912. *Oscar C. Kuehn, Missouri Historical Society.*

Ulysses dubbed it Hardscrabble. His youngest son, Jesse, said Ulysses "bestowed it in humorous recognition and defiance of the conditions father understood and voluntarily faced." Some authors suggest that Ulysses gave it that name as a subtle dig at neighbors who gave high-sounding names to rather plain homes in imitation of more extensive and expensive Southern plantations—for example, White Haven or Wish-ton-wish.

Julia had moments when she couldn't understand why they couldn't have stayed and enjoyed the comforts of Wish-ton-wish. Yet she worked hard to make Hardscrabble cozy and warm. Julia's friend Minerva Blow, wife of prominent St. Louisan Henry Blow, gushed that it was better than a grand city home. It was spotless, with engravings on the wall, books lying about and had a warm family atmosphere.

In her life as a farmer's wife, Julia still had enslaved people to help her with work around the house. Besides being in charge of creating a comfortable home (despite the rustic nature of the log cabin), Julia also kept a flower garden that brightened and softened the home, inside and out.

She was keeper of the chickens, and Ulysses brought her all the new breeds—Shanghais, Brahmas and Bantams. Julia named each one. She observed that the roosters, both foreign and domestic, would often find a choice tidbit of food and call the hens to share it. As the females converged, the rooster ate it himself.

Julia even took a turn—meaning one—at churning butter. The servant responsible for butter making was let go, and it was churning day. Julia looked up directions in her cookbook, took up the churning dash and sent her "girl" to the spring for water to cool the butter. The girl said she would only be gone ten minutes and Julia would be tired before she returned, but once she started the churning (up and down with the dasher), she could not stop, or the butter would be ruined. The girl returned within ten minutes, just as Julia's arms were barely able to move the dasher. When the servant took the lid off, she remarked the fairies must have come and helped with the churning because it was full of butter.

Ulysses had his lowest moments when away from his wife and children. Yet Julia suffered some of her lowest times during their short sojourn at Hardscrabble. In one instance, she claims a visit from the fairies (perhaps the same who helped her churn) saved her. Julia was feeling quite blue, rare for her, when an even deeper depression, like a black cloud, enveloped her. She said aloud, "Is this my destiny? Is this my destiny? These crude, not to say rough surroundings; to eat, to sleep, to wake again and again to the same—oh sad is me!" Julia said the dark cloud disappeared upon this exclamation, and a silvery light hovered about her. She heard—was it a fairy visit?—"No, no this is not your destiny. Cheer up, be happy now, make the best of this. Up and be doing for your dear ones." Julia felt this was her lowest point, and never again did she let herself sink into despair, even in harder times she met in the future. Going forward, she "had no fear and did not lose my courage."

The winter of 1856–57 was hard for the Grant family. They'd lived in their Hardscrabble cabin for only three months. Although they led a simple life, money was short. Grant worked hard clearing additional acreage and selling the wood for extra cash but informed his father he could not buy seed to plant his acreage come spring without a loan. There is no record of Jesse sending money, but Ulysses managed to buy seed and plant the fields. Julia was grieving the loss of her mother in January 1857, and her father, lonely without Ellen, was being especially difficult. In the spring, Julia fell ill. They moved back to White Haven.

On December 28, 1856, Ulysses wrote an optimistic letter to his father. "Evry day I like farming better and I do not doubt but that money is to be made at it." In the past year, the land Dent had given them "was not half tended because I had but one span of horses, and one hand, and we had to do all the work of the place, living at a distance too, all the hawling for my building, and take wood to the city for the support of the family."

He couldn't plant all the potatoes he wanted, but he sold 225 bushels of potatoes and had another 125 bushels ready to plant next year. He also had twenty-five acres of winter wheat. Ulysses had big plans for 1857. He was going to plant twenty acres of potatoes, five acres of sweet potatoes and five or six acres of cabbages, pickles, beets and melons and keep a wagon going to market every day with a load of wood to support the family until he could farm "independently." His vision of becoming a "well-to-do Missouri farmer" seemed ever more possible.

But there was one more thing he wanted to mention to Jesse. "If I had an opportunity of getting about $500.00 for a year at 10 pr. cent I have no doubt but it would be a great advantage to me." His father did not take the hint, forcing Ulysses to ask for a loan more directly in his next letter. On February 7, 1857, he wrote:

> *Spring is now approaching when farmers require not only to till the soil, but to have the wherewith to till it, and to seed it. For two years I have been compelled to farm without either of these facilities.... To this end I am going to make this last appeal to you. I do this because, when I was in Ky. You volunteered to give a Thousand dollars, to commence with and because there was no one else to whom I could, with the same propriety, apply. It is always usual for parents to give their children assistance in beginning life (and I am only beginning, though thirty five years of age, nearly) and what I ask is not much. But what I do ask is that you lend, or borrow for, me Five hundred dollars, for two years at 10 pr. cent payable annually, or semmi annually if you choose, and with this if I do not go on prosperously I shall ask no more from you.*

But the year was not to be a happy one.

8

POLITICS AND SLAVERY

By the time Ulysses left the army and returned to Missouri, the politics of slavery had heated up for the third time in thirty years, this time not to be headed off by compromises.

In 1821, Missouri was admitted as a slave state and Maine as a free state. The Missouri Compromise settled the question of slavery in the Louisiana Purchase territories by prohibiting slavery below Missouri's southern border—the 36° 30' line. But, as Thomas Jefferson recognized, this was "a reprieve only, not a final sentence." The question of the extension of slavery into new territories erupted again after the United States acquired large swaths of new land from Mexico after the conclusion of that war. The Compromise of 1850 calmed the disputes, but it was only another reprieve.

The Election of 1856

Senator Stephen A. Douglas introduced the Kansas-Nebraska Act of 1854, providing for "the questions pertaining to slavery in the territories, and in the new states to be formed therefrom, are to be left to the decision of the people residing therein, through their representatives." The Kansas-Nebraska Act repealed the Missouri Compromise and threatened to undo the Compromise of 1850. Rather than solve the problem of the extension of slavery to the territories, however, it made it worse.

Northern antislavery politicians condemned the act as "a gross violation of a sacred pledge; as a criminal betrayal of precious rights; as part and parcel of an atrocious plot to exclude from a vast unoccupied region immigrants from the Old World and free laborers from our own States, and convert it into a dreary region of despotism, inhabited by masters and slaves." Congress approved the bill narrowly in the House and by a greater margin in the Senate. President Franklin Pierce signed the act into law on May 30, 1854.

Within months, six hundred antislavery settlers had founded the town of Lawrence on the Kaw River. They were sponsored by groups such as the Massachusetts Emigrant Aid Society, known later as the New England Emigrant Aid Society. Despite the name, most of these settlers came from the Ohio Valley states of Illinois, Indiana and Ohio—only about 5 percent came from New England. With a shorter trip across the nearby state line, proslavery Missourians founded Leavenworth within two weeks of the law's passage.

Proslavery and antislavery settlers drafted competing constitutions. The proslavery candidate for the territorial delegate to Congress won thanks to 1,700 Missourians who crossed the state line the night before to vote. John Brown—Jesse Grant's friend from his younger days in Ohio—migrated to Kansas in 1855 seeking "to help defeat SATAN and his legions." Kansas and the nation headed toward a violent confrontation.

In early May 1856, Border Ruffians from Missouri sacked Lawrence, burning the Free State Hotel to the ground and destroying two abolitionist newspapers. On May 19 and 20, fire-breathing Massachusetts Senator Charles Sumner delivered a speech titled "The Crime Against Kansas," in which he attacked the Kansas-Nebraska Act and its co-sponsors, Stephen A. Douglas and South Carolina Senator Andrew Butler, in the harshest and most insulting terms. On May 22, Butler's cousin Congressman Preston Brooks entered the Senate floor and beat Sumner severely with a cane. Sumner did not return from his injuries for years. On the night of May 24, John Brown, three of his sons and four other men murdered five men near Pottawatomie, Kansas, in what became known as the Pottawatomie Massacre.

Amid this turmoil, which earned the name "Bleeding Kansas," there was a presidential election. As he cut and sold cordwood and built Hardscrabble, where did Ulysses stand on the candidates?

Jesse Grant was a Whig. Ulysses was a Whig, too, although he gave little thought to party politics while still in the army. Whigs opposed the

Mexican War and the annexation of additional territory from Mexico, seeing it as a bid to increase slavery. In a very Whiggish passage in his *Personal Memoirs*, Ulysses wrote that the army was sent to Texas to provoke the Mexican government to attack and provide an excuse for invasion. He regarded the war

> *as one of the most unjust ever waged by a stronger against a weaker nation.... The occupation, separation, and annexation were, from the inception of the movement to its final consummation, a conspiracy to acquire territory out of which slave states might be formed for the American Union.*

However, the Whig Party did not survive the controversy over the Kansas-Nebraska Act. Many Northern Whigs ultimately joined the nascent Republican Party for the 1856 presidential election. Southern Whigs gravitated to the equally new American Party, better known to history as the Know Nothings. They were supposed to be an alternative for voters who could not support the antislavery views espoused by the Republicans and did not want to associate themselves with the proslavery Democratic Party. But the Know Nothings had their own set of prejudices—the party was rabidly anti-Catholic and anti-immigrant, arguing that they were bringing anti-American notions into government.

Ulysses admitted in his *Personal Memoirs* that he flirted with the Know Nothing Party. He accepted an invitation to join and was initiated into a local lodge. He attended one meeting and never went back. In retrospect, Ulysses made "no apologies for having been for one week a member of the American party; for I still think native-born citizens of the United States should have as much protection, as many privileges in their native country,

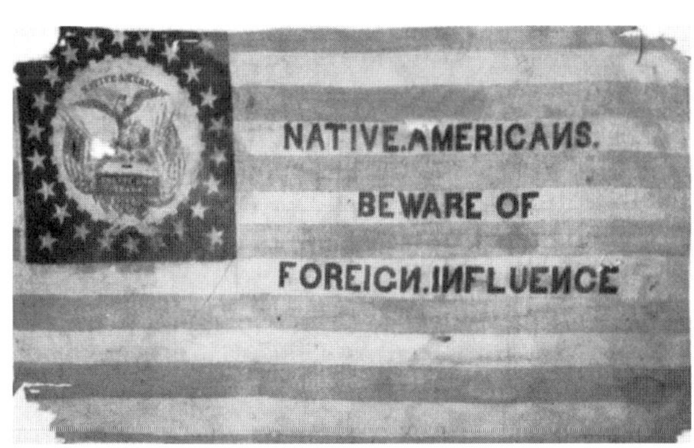

Know Nothing Flag. *https://www.latinamericanstudies.org/immigration/know-nothing-flag.jpg.*

as those who voluntarily select it for a home." But he opposed the party's secret oaths and its attempt to set up laws that were binding above the government's laws. He made plain that he also opposed any party seeking to curtail freedom of thought and religion. Ulysses's nativist tendencies would, however, emerge again a few years later before he left Missouri.

The presidential candidates in 1856 were Millard Fillmore of the American Party, former army officer and the "Pathfinder" John C. Frémont of the newly organized Republican Party and James Buchanan of the Democratic Party. Ulysses decided he could not vote for Fillmore because, despite some sympathy for the party's views, he quickly came to regard it as a secret sect that set itself above the laws of the land. Ulysses chose to vote for Buchanan. He later joked, "I voted for Buchanan because I didn't know him and voted against Frémont because I did know him." That wasn't exactly true—Frémont wasn't even on the ballot in Missouri in 1856.

Whatever their differences on other matters, Ulysses and Colonel Dent supported the same candidate, although likely for far different reasons. In his *Personal Memoirs*, Ulysses explained his vote for Buchanan as a vote to avoid war:

> *It was evident to my mind that the election of a Republican President in 1856 meant the secession of all the Slave states, and rebellion. Under these circumstances I preferred the success of a candidate whose election would prevent or postpone secession, to seeing the country plunged into a war the end of which no man could foretell. With a Democrat elected by the unanimous vote of the Slave States, there could be no pretext for secession for four years. I very much hoped that the passions of the people would subside in that time, and the catastrophe averted altogether; if it was not, I believed the country would be better prepared to receive the shock and to resist it.*

LIBERATOR

Ulysses justified his vote for the proslavery candidate in 1856 as motivated by a desire to preserve the Union, not as support for slavery. He grew up in a family where his father was against slavery to the point that he vowed not to live in a slave state (a vow he later broke). Ulysses's mother disapproved of Julia's dependence on enslaved labor to run her household. And yet, Ulysses lived in a slave state on a farm owned by a slaveowner; he was married to a woman who had slaves as servants, and at some point, he owned a slave himself. This raises a question that historians have pondered ever since: What were his beliefs while living in Missouri about *the* divisive issue of the day—slavery?

Ulysses left no definitive answer to that question. In his *Personal Memoirs*, he does not comment on his prewar attitudes toward the peculiar institution. Some historians point to interviews conducted after his death with people who knew him during that period. For example, Louisa Boggs, wife of Ulysses's 1859 business partner, said he "was no hand to manage negroes" because "he was not a slavery man." Mary Robinson, a formerly enslaved woman who was the Dent family cook, recalled, "Grant was a very kind man to those who worked for him, and he always said that he wanted to give his wife's slaves their freedom as soon as he was able." Some have regarded these comments with skepticism because they came after Ulysses's death and were possibly, if not likely, solicited to fortify his reputation as the soldier who led the fight to free the slaves. Others have pointed out that Ulysses worked alongside enslaved men in clearing his land, cutting and loading cordwood and farming White Haven. It was, however, common in Missouri—unlike on plantations in the Deep South—for white men to work in the fields with their enslaved farmhands, especially on farms with few bondsmen.

As Nicholas Sacco points out, Ulysses was one of three appraisers appointed to place a value on three slaves in the estate of his neighbor Richard Wells. And of course, he lived on the farm and in the household of the ardently proslavery Frederick Dent Sr., who at one time served on the finance committee of the St. Louis Anti-Abolitionist Society.

On the other hand, Ulysses and Julia were also friends with Henry Taylor Blow and his wife, Minerva. The Blow family brought a slave named Dred Scott to Missouri in the 1830s. They sold Scott to Dr. John Emerson, who later, on assignment with the army, took Scott to the free state of Illinois and to Fort Snelling at St. Paul, then in the free territory of Wisconsin (now Minnesota). There, Dred married Harriet Robinson. When Dred and Harriet Robinson Scott filed their freedom suits in St. Louis in 1846, the Blows provided financial support while the case made its tortuous course through the state and federal courts. After the decision in *Dred Scott v. Sandford* in 1857, Taylor Blow purchased the Scotts and freed them, providing the $1,000 bond required by Missouri law for emancipated slaves.

Ulysses did not vote in the 1860 election because he had not lived in Illinois long enough, but he supported Douglas. Immediately after the commencement of the war by the firing on Fort Sumter, Ulysses made clear to his father-in-law that now was the time to save and protect the Union and slavery be damned.

> *No impartial man can conceal from himself the fact that in all these troubles the South have been the aggressors and the Administration has stood purely on the defensive, more on the defensive than she would dared to have done but for her consiousness of strength and the certainty of right prevailing in the end.*
>
> *In all this I can but see the doom of Slavery. The North do not want, nor will they want, to interfere with the institution. But they will refuse for all time to give it protection unless the South shall return soon to their allegiance, and then too this disturbance will give such an impetus to the production of their staple, cotton, in other parts of the world that they can never recover the controll of the market again for that comodity. This will reduce the value of negroes so much that they will never be worth fighting over again.*

Two days later, Ulysses wrote to his father that he owed an obligation to his country to offer his services because it had educated him on military matters. Moreover, he added:

> *Whatever may have been my political opinions before I have but one sentiment now. That is we have a Government, and laws and a flag and they must all be sustained. There are but two parties now, Traitors & Patriots and I want hereafter to be ranked with the latter, and I trust the stronger party.*

After he rejoined the army in 1861, military orders overruled whatever Ulysses's private thoughts were about slavery. Missouri and Kentucky remained, after all, slave states. Orders were to return runaway slaves to their masters, or at least the loyal ones. That sometimes caused conflict with his own troops. Ulysses chastised the commander of Fort Holt in Kentucky for refusing to allow a slaveowner to search for slaves alleged to have taken refuge there. "I do not want the Army to be used as negro cat[c]hers, but still less do I want it used as a cloak to cover their escape."

As the war progressed, however, it became apparent to him that the destruction of slavery was going to be an essential part of defeating the Confederacy. Slavery was and had to be doomed. In Kristopher Teeters's characterization, Grant and many Union officers became "practical liberators." As Federal armies penetrated the South, thousands of the formerly enslaved fled their bondage for the safety of Union lines. The Federals took them in as laborers, cooks and servants. Emancipating the enslaved of the South was an important military measure because it weakened the Confederacy by depriving them of much-needed manpower. Ultimately, the Union enlisted thousands of able-bodied Black men as soldiers to take a more direct role in the victory.

After the issue of the Emancipation Proclamation, Ulysses wrote to his patron in Congress, Elihu Washburne, that "I never was an Abolitionist, [n]ot even what could be called antislavery" before the war. By 1863, Ulysses told President Lincoln that "I have given the subject of the arming the negro my hearty support." Unlike other generals—most notably William Sherman—Ulysses proved willing to use U.S. Colored Troops as an important part of his army.

So, what *was* Ulysses's attitude toward slavery while living in Missouri? The evidence is scant and ambiguous. The best answer is that given by Nicholas Sacco. Grant and his family benefited from slavery in the 1850s. He did not express strong convictions either in support of or against slavery, at least none that have ever been recorded or observed. Perhaps Ulysses approached the issue as he did the change of his name at West Point or the issue of emancipation after the war started. He accepted it as a practical matter because he could not then change it, and being with his family was more important than politics.

9

LEAVING MISSOURI

Ulysses looked forward to 1857 with optimism, tempered by his need for cash to buy machinery and seed to till the land. Whether Jesse Grant responded to Ulysses's request for $500 for this purpose, we don't know. Emma said that Jesse had given him $1,000 the year before, and others claimed that Jesse had given him twice as much. With or without Jesse's financial assistance, Ulysses planted wheat, corn, oats, potatoes, sweet potatoes, melons and cabbages.

The Panic of 1857

What began on a hopeful note ended sourly. Ulysses expected a yield of four to five hundred bushels of wheat but realized only seventy-five bushels. The short wheat harvest didn't matter much because the Panic of 1857 hit every farmer hard, with wheat prices dropping by more than 60 percent from prior years, largely due to the reopening of the Russian wheat market to Europe at the end of the Crimean War. Financial markets fell precipitously as well. Banks collapsed, companies went bankrupt and many farmers lost their holdings to foreclosure. Ulysses was able to make some money from cordwood sales, potatoes and other lesser crops.

Yet he found himself still in need of cash. On December 23, 1857, he pawned his gold watch and chain for twenty-two dollars. The story is that he used the money to buy Christmas presents, but other than the transaction date, there is no evidence to support that O. Henry–esque tale. We don't know what he used the money for or if he redeemed the watch later. However, it suggests that times were tight in the Grant and Dent household at the end of 1857. Times were to get worse.

On March 21, 1858, Ulysses wrote to his sister Mary about the family and the farm. He and Julia rented out Hardscrabble. Colonel Dent and Emma moved to the Dent home in St. Louis at Fourth and Cerre. Ulysses took over management of White Haven proper. Once again, he was optimistic about the upcoming summer. "The Spring opened finely for farming," he wrote, "but I shall wait until the crops are gathered before I make any predictions." He had three enslaved men, two of whom he hired and one "of Mr. Dent's" (possibly William Jones) to work with him on the farm. Ulysses planned to plant "20 acres of potatoes, 20 of corn, 25 of oats 50 of wheat, 25 of meadow, some clover, Hungarian grass and other smaller products all of which require labor before they are got into market, and the money realized upon them."

There were a few clouds on the horizon. Ulysses told Mary that a bank loan he owed came due in April, "and I don't see now that I shall have the money." This might have been the loan the Colonel had taken out years before that was still unpaid. In June, Colonel Dent borrowed even more money, this time $4,800 from Harry Boggs, secured by another mortgage on White Haven. The funds were used to make payments on the prior loan and for farm expenses.

The summer of 1858 brought new woes. A bad spell of cold weather in June damaged the crops. What was worse, the entire family fell ill. Son Fred suffered from typhoid, leaving him deaf for some time. Young Fred was so sick with typhoid that Jesse made the trip from Covington to see him, fearing that he was on his deathbed. Ulysses had a lengthy relapse of his childhood malaria. Likely, his farmhands suffered as well (Little says seven of them also had typhoid), and in any event, Ulysses was not there to supervise them. Fred and the rest of the family recovered. What else could go wrong? Finally, Julia asked her father if there might not be a place of employment for her husband in the city.

The news from 1858 was not all bad. Julia's and Ulysses's youngest son, Jesse Root Grant II, was born on February 6, 1858, at White Haven.

Grant as Businessman

By October, Ulysses, in consultation with Colonel Dent, had decided to sell the farm's equipment and stock, rent the cleared land (about 450 acres) and sell 400 acres at the north end of the property, including Hardscrabble. The farming experiment was over. Ulysses apparently consulted his father about a job with his business, but just a salaried position. Ulysses wanted to own his own business at some point because "There is a pleasure in knowing that one's income depends somewhat upon his own exertions and business capacity, that cannot be felt when so much and no more is coming in, regardless of the success of the business engaged in or the manner in which it is done." Despite these discussions, Ulysses and his family did not move to Covington. There is nothing in Ulysses's correspondence to explain why this proposal fell through, but Julia was likely against it because she believed (with some reason) that his family did not like her.

Sometime in the fall of 1858, Ulysses ran into Harry Boggs. Colonel Dent was Boggs's uncle. Ulysses told him, "The old gentleman is trying to persuade me to go into business with someone and he speaks of you. He thinks I could learn the details, and that my large acquaintance among army officers would bring enough additional customers to make it support both

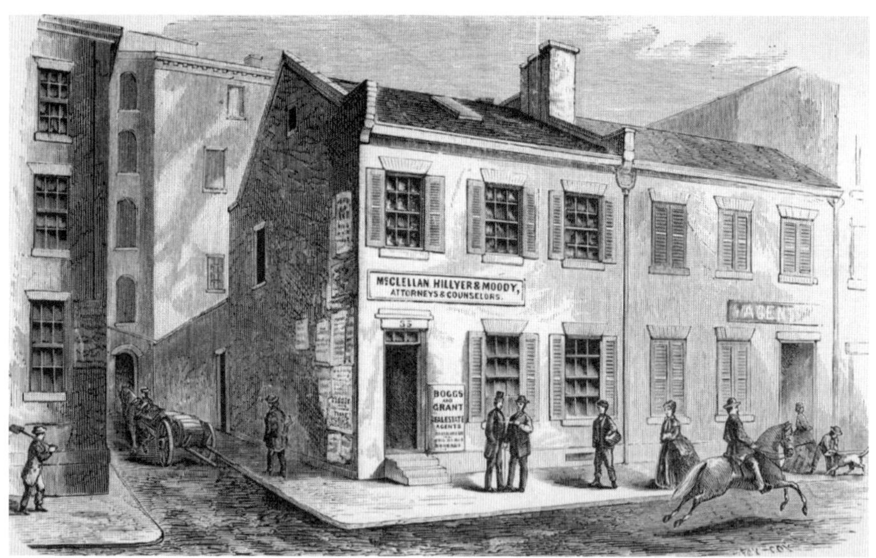

Boggs and Grant office, 1859. *From Albert D. Richardson,* A Personal History of Ulysses S. Grant and a Sketch of Schuyler Colfax *(1868).*

our families." Boggs agreed. They formed the firm of Boggs & Grant dealing in real estate, loans and rent collection. They shared offices in a building at 35 Pine Street with the law firm of McClellan, Hillyer and Moody. In January 1859, Ulysses moved in with Harry and Louisa Boggs on Fifteenth Street. He slept in an unheated room for a couple of months with only a bed and a chair. He spent the weekdays in the city and traveled to White Haven to be with Julia and the children on weekends.

In March, Julia, the four children and Julia's four slaves joined Ulysses at a rented house at Seventh and Lynch Streets. Julia was relieved they were not moving to Kentucky; their lifestyles were so unlike Ulysses's family. This new home was near the river, away from the fashionable district where she had once lived. They were out of the orbit of Julia's society associates, such as the O'Fallons. However, they remained friendly, unlike some of their acquaintances who were becoming more politically Southern in their views. The house was two miles from Ulysses's office, and he was often late for work, claiming Julia was so busy with the children that breakfast had been late. For the first time, Julia was too busy with her four children and too worried about her husband's unhappiness and ill health to be concerned with social engagement.

The children had to leave their pets behind at White Haven, including a Newfoundland dog named Leo. Colonel Dent suggested he buy the dog and keep him in the country. The boys were against this plan until their grandfather convinced them Leo would be much happier with room to roam and run. Colonel Dent asked how much they wanted for the dog; the first demand was $10. The Colonel refused and asked for a more reasonable sale price. Finally, they agreed on $2.50, and Colonel Dent promptly paid.

The next morning, Julia couldn't find the boys anywhere, and one of the enslaved, young Johnny, hadn't shown up asking what he needed to do. When Julia heard a commotion coming from the backyard, she found her sons, along with a number of dogs they had tied to the fence. When asked what in the world the dogs were doing there, Buck answered Johnny had caught them all, and they planned to sell them to their grandfather for $2.50 each. The dogs, on Julia's command, were freed.

The boys were sent to school, and Julia set up her new city house in the same comfortable manner she'd always done with their homes. It wasn't long before she realized Ulysses was unhappy.

In October, the family moved to larger quarters at 1008 Barton Street, where they remained until they left Missouri permanently in May 1860. The transaction to acquire the Barton Street home was a complicated

Grant residence at 1008 Barton, St. Louis. The building still stands; this photograph dates to about 1940. *Missouri Historical Society*.

one. Because of Colonel Dent's casual ways with property, neither Julia nor Ulysses had title to Hardscrabble. Therefore, Colonel Dent deeded Hardscrabble to Joseph White in return for his deed to the house in the city. White gave Ulysses and Julia six promissory notes, one for $3,000 payable in five years and five for $180 each payable annually. White also executed a mortgage on Hardscrabble in favor of Dent to secure payment of the $3,000 note. By 1865, Julia succeeded to the ownership of the note and mortgage.

As a result, the ownership of Hardscrabble fell into litigation that lasted for years. White made his payments on the promissory note until sometime during the Civil War, when he defaulted. Because Ulysses was busy fighting the war, he asked Julia to purchase the property at the foreclosure auction. Julia was successful and, for whatever reason, agreed to let White stay on the property and pay her rent. Again, he did not pay and would not leave. The Grants sued and lost the first round. They appealed. In 1867, Julia gave a deposition from Washington outlining the contract she made with White and denying that she had agreed to return all the promissory notes at the end of the lease. The Grants won the second round when the court reversed the judgment and awarded them damages. White appealed, and the Grants won the third round, too. White argued that Julia was a "femme covert" (married woman) and therefore could not legally sign the contract. On March 30, 1868, the Missouri Supreme Court ruled unanimously in favor of the Grants. They rejected the claim that married women could not legally execute contracts, affirming the principle that women in Missouri, married or single, had the legal right to sign contracts in their own name or as agents of their husbands and the right to own property. Although Julia was never one to agitate for equal rights for women, she won an important right for the women of her home state.

Harry and Louisa Boggs and Josiah McClellan were, like Colonel Dent, strongly proslavery. William Hillyer, McClellan's law partner, had been a Know Nothing. Hillyer later recalled that Ulysses and his office mates had extensive discussions about the issues of the day without specifying their content except to say that Ulysses adamantly opposed secession and liked to tell war stories about his experiences in Mexico. Hillyer later served on Ulysses's staff when he was promoted to brigadier and major general. Another group member was Charles Johnson, who was reading law at the firm. Johnson later became lieutenant governor of Missouri; one of Frank James's defense counsels at his murder trial in Gallatin, Missouri; a criminal law professor at Washington University Law School; and the defense counsel for Lee ("Stack Lee") Shelton, whose shooting of Billy Lyons was the inspiration for the 1959 hit song "Stagger Lee."

Ulysses's extensive contacts at Jefferson Barracks did not pan out. He was assigned mainly clerical work. His business colleagues and family didn't think he was cut out to sell real estate and collect past-due rents. Julia agreed, although she probably kept her opinion to herself. "I cannot imagine how my dear husband ever thought of going into such a business, as he could never collect a penny that was owed him if his debtors, and he had several, only expressed regret."

Shortly after Julia and the family moved to Barton Street, Ulysses went to the St. Louis County Courthouse and filed the following deed of manumission:

> *Know all persons by these presents, that I Ulysses S Grant of the City & County of St Louis in the State of Missouri, for divers good and valuable considerations me hereunto moving, do hereby emancipate and set free from Slavery my negro man William, sometimes called William Jones (Jones) of Mullato complexion, aged about thirty-five years, and about five feet seven inches in height and being the same slave purchased by me*

Know all persons by these presents, that I Ulysses S Grant of the City & County of St Louis in the State of Missouri, for divers good and valuable considerations me hereunto moving, do hereby emancipate and set free from Slavery my Negro man William, sometimes called William Jones (Jones) of Mullatto complexion, aged about thirty-five years, and about five feet seven inches in height and being the same slave purchased by me of Frederick Dent — And I do hereby manumit, emancipate & set free said William from slavery forever

In testimony Whereof I hereto set my hand & seal at St Louis this day of March AD 1859

U. S. Grant (Seal)

Witness

J. W. McClellan

W. S. Hillyer

In St Louis Circuit Court February Term 1859

March 29 1859

Be it remembered that on this twenty-ninth day of March 1859 In Open Court came U S Grant who is personally known to the Court to be the same person wh. se name is subscribed to the foregoing instrument of writing as a party thereto, and he acknowledged the same to be his act and deed for the purposes therein mentioned Which said acknowledgment is entered on the record of the Court of that day

In Testimony Whereof I hereto set my hand And affix the seal of said Court at office in the City of St Louis the day and year above written

Stephen Reid Clerk

COMPLIMENTS OF THE MISSOURI HISTORICAL SOCIETY

William Jones manumission signed by Ulysses S. Grant, 1859. *Missouri Historical Society.*

of Frederick Dent—And I do hereby manumit, emancipate & set free said William from slavery forever

In testimony Whereof I hereto set my hand & seal at St Louis this [twenty-ninth] *day of March A D 1859*

Witnesses *U.S. Grant (Seal)*
J G McClellan
W.S. Hillyer

Ulysses never explained his decision to free William Jones. We can speculate that once he moved to the City, leased White Haven and sold Hardscrabble, he no longer needed Jones as a farmhand and Julia didn't need him to run the household. Ulysses could have sold Jones for a substantial price in 1859, or he could have hired him out—William was an experienced, able-bodied farmer. And yet, he chose to free the man.

We don't know what happened to William Jones after he was emancipated either. Being a free Black person did not mean that they were free of all restrictions on their life. Freed slaves were required by Missouri law to post a bond ranging from $100 to $1,000. It is unlikely that Ulysses's generosity extended to posting a bond for his former slave, given his personal financial situation. Nicholas Sacco has attempted to trace Jones's post-slavery life with limited success. The 1860 City Directory lists a William Jones, but other documents such as the 1860 Census did not confirm that this was the same man. He found court records showing that a William Jones was arrested in May 1861 and whipped for failing to have his freedom papers. Jones's life story was, as Sacco wrote, a mystery.

A Failed Job Application

By the summer of 1859, it became clear that Ulysses needed to seek other employment. Jesse suggested that Ulysses apply for a professorship of mathematics at Washington University. Ulysses pointed out that the vacancy was already filled. And besides, Isaac Quinby, the best mathematician in his West Point class and an experienced professor, applied for the job unsuccessfully. Ulysses wouldn't have had a chance even if he tried.

Providentially, the post of St. Louis County engineer came open at $1,500 per year. As a West Point graduate, Ulysses was well qualified for a job that required supervising the construction and maintenance of roads and bridges. On August 15, 1859, Ulysses submitted his application to the Board of County Commissioners supported by letters of recommendation from two of his classmates at West Point: John J. Reynolds (professor of engineering at Washington University) and David M. Frost (later commander of the Missouri Militia captured by Nathaniel Lyon in the controversial Camp Jackson Affair in May 1861). In addition, thirty-four other men endorsed Ulysses's application. These included the three lawyers whose office he shared and prominent St. Louisans John O'Fallon and Taylor Blow.

Despite the backing of these worthies, Ulysses was not confident about getting the appointment. Slavery politics entered into the equation. Three of the five commissioners—Dr. William Taussig, John H. Lightner and Benjamin Farrar (later Union provost marshal in St. Louis and commander of a U.S. Colored Infantry regiment)—were Free-Soilers. Two commissioners—Alton Easton (after whom the town of Alton, Illinois, was named) and Judge Peregrine Tibbets—were Democrats. The vote 3–2 was for Charles E. Salomon, a German American immigrant and later a colonel in the Union army.

Supposedly, Ulysses sat outside the courthouse, awaiting the decision. When a friend told him that he was beaten, Ulysses replied, "Yes, and by a Dutchman." The loss of the job to a "Dutchman" still rankled Ulysses years later when he wrote in his *Personal Memoirs* that his opponent "had the advantage of birth over me (he was a citizen by adoption) and carried off the prize." He wrote a disgusted letter to Jesse after the decision:

> *You may judge from the result of the action of the County Commissioners that I am strongly identified with the Democratic party! Such is not the case. I never voted an out and out Democratic ticket in my life. I voted for Buch. for President to defeat Freemont but not because he was my first choice. In all other elections I have universally selected the candidates that in my estimation, were the best fitted for the different offices and it never happens that such men are all arrayed on one side. The strongest friend I had in the Board of Comrs. is a F.S. but opposition between parties is so strong that he would not vote for any one, no matter how friendly, unless at least one of his own party would go with him. The F.S. party felt themselves bound to provide for one of their own party who was defeated for the office of County Engineer; a Dutchman who came to the West as an Assistant Surveyor upon the publick lands and who has held an office ever since. There is,*

> *I believe, but one paying office in the County held by an American unless you except the office of Sheriff which is held by a Frenchman who speaks broken English but was born here.*

Dr. Taussig, Ulysses's neighbor who voted against him, confirmed the suspicions years later. The commissioners weren't convinced of Ulysses's loyalty to the Union, primarily because he lived with Colonel Dent and was associated with persons like McClellan, Boggs and Frost such that "the shadow of their disloyalty necessarily fell on him."

Ulysses worked briefly at the U.S. Customs House, but it was apparent by early 1860 that he would have to go back to his father for a job. Julia was more supportive this time, urging him to go to Covington. Jesse sent him to work at his store in Galena, Illinois, run by Ulysses's brother Simpson. Before they moved in May 1860, Ulysses and Julia rented their home on Barton, and Julia hired out her four slaves. "Papa was not willing they should go with me to Galena," Julia said later, "saying the place might not suit us after all, and if I took them they would, of course, be free, 'and you know, sister, you cannot do without servants.'"

Ulysses and Julia Grant returned to Missouri from time to time, but they would not live there again.

Many historians consider Ulysses's and Julia's life a failure during this time. However, Julia's sister Emma disagreed. Emma said, when commenting on how others viewed Grant's farming days as a failure,

> *It is true fame had not yet come to him, nor had riches, but he had never shown greater strength of character, greater fortitude under adverse circumstances, nor more determination that he did at this time…* [during] *these simple days of hard work on his Missouri farm. If earning and winning the reputation of being one of the best farmers in a country of farmers is to be a failure, then perhaps, the ex-army officer at that period was a failure. He worked early and late; his crops were put in always at the right time, and cultivated at the right time; they turned out better than the crops of his neighbors.…Grant turned farmer after he left the army, not because he couldn't do anything else, but because he wanted to be a farmer. That he later left the farm and became a store-keeper was not due to any vacillation of character, but to ill finances.*

Julia agreed with her sister's assessment. In her *Memoirs*, she writes, "Ulys was really very successful at farming. His crops yielded well—that is, much better than Papa's, but not as much as he anticipated from his calculations on paper—and I was a splendid farmer's wife." Her children do not recall the time in Missouri as a time of "poverty."

The time spent in Missouri had a profound influence on Ulysses. It continued to show his belief in and ability to work hard. He built a strong family that would give him confidence and comfort in the stressful days of the war to come. He also built a relationship with the Dents, worked with enslaved and learned their worth, freed the only enslaved man he ever owned as a precursor to a greater emancipation of African Americans and developed some of the important political beliefs that colored his military work and political life. His struggles made him stronger, and his experiences made him more sympathetic to the public and voters in his future.

10

STARTING OVER IN GALENA AND THE COMING OF THE CIVIL WAR

Ulysses and Julia arrived in Galena, Illinois, in May 1860. Galena was a prosperous town of fifteen thousand in the middle of a lead mining belt a few miles from the Mississippi River. Ulysses went to work in his father's leather goods store as an employee, hoping to eventually become a part owner. He was found primarily in the store's back office, keeping the accounts, processing orders and taking in hides. His salary was $800, although, in that first year, he drew $1,500, an overage he paid back once he was in the army. The store was doing well, with annual revenues of about $100,000.

Family Life in a New Home

The Grants moved into a two-story brick home located on High Street, no doubt named after the high bluff where it sat. Two hundred feet of wooden steps led to the house from the main street. They shared the house with Ulysses's brother Simpson to save on expenses. Rent was $125 a year.

Julia had one servant, Jennie, to help her around the house. She set about making the home comfortable and teaching the girl how to make Maryland biscuits, a family favorite. Unfortunately, as Julia recalled when the biscuits failed, she had never actually made them herself. Yet she blamed their failure on the flour. When the hired girl made delicious bread for the family, Ulysses pointed out Julia must have found better flour. Julia recalls Jennie doing all the housework herself, not letting Julia even help with the dishes. "Oh, please, madam," Jennie said, "do not interfere with me or my work."

During that first year in Galena, Julia socialized little. She was busy settling in and handling family matters. Julia had four children to take care of. Each was growing into their own person and believed they were their parents' favorite: Fred because he was eldest, Ulysses (Buck) because he bore his father's name, Nellie because she was the only girl and Jesse because he was youngest.

Fred was a storyteller. He often recounted his feats of prowess, less often those of his defeats. When he was defeated, he added a verse about how he was sure to get even.

Buck had curls to his waist until he was eight years old—at Julia's insistence. When she finally gave in to his demands to cut them, he announced the "shearing," as Julia called it, to all his schoolmates. They showed up at the appointed time, all wanting one of "Deliciouses" curls.

Ulysses and Julia Grant house, Galena, Illinois. *Carol M. Highsmith, Library of Congress.*

Julia, 1861. *Library of Congress.*

Buck was also kindhearted. He had a friend, a younger boy, he "adopted." He told his mother that the boy had no parents, only an older sister who didn't take good care of him. Buck brought him home and gave him dinner on cold days. He often acted as a protector to smaller boys he encountered.

Nellie spent much time engaged in games and playing with her brothers until she was in danger of becoming a tomboy. Like Julia, she was a great pet of her father's.

And Jesse was the baby—an adventurous baby. One day, on awakening from a nap, he decided to try on a pair of his father's boots. The results, when Jesse came down the stairs, were disastrous. He broke off four of his teeth.

Julia insisted the children always look their best, much to the boys' chagrin. The boys wore waistcoats buttoned to their short pants, and she took special care with Nellie's curls. Each evening before their father came home from work, Julia made sure the children were clean and neat. And she always made sure they attended the First Methodist Church of Galena.

In the evenings, after the children were in bed, Ulysses read aloud, first the newspapers, then a book, while Julia mended the children's clothes.

Julia felt comfortable in Galena with her family around her and making acquaintances she found pleasant. The Grants were happy.

THE SPRING OF '61

Politics were in the hearts and on the minds of all those in Galena and elsewhere across the country in the spring of 1861. Ulysses played his political cards as close to his chest as he did his poker cards, while Julia was more vocal. She felt that states should have the right to secede—fueled no doubt by her father's fervent belief in this—yet it was the duty of the government to prevent "dismemberment of the Union." Ulysses pointed out that she was somewhat inconsistent in her sentiments.

Once Fort Sumter was fired on and patriotism ran rampant in Galena, Julia felt she should help somehow and attended a sewing circle. By the time she arrived, all the tasks had been handed out. The woman in charge asked Julia if she could knit, and Julia said she could. After all, she had knit small things for her children. She was given wool and needles to make socks. Could she finish in a week? Much to her embarrassment, Julia had no idea where to start and admitted as much. She was given a lesser task, which she completed, but Julia never attended the sewing circle again.

11

THE CIVIL WAR

When the war finally came, Galena enthusiastically supported the raising of volunteers. Because of his military experience, Ulysses chaired the initial meeting and described what the men who signed up could expect. It was a sobering talk: he spoke of long marches in the rain, sleeping on the cold ground and obeying orders—even ones they might disagree with—without hesitation. At the meeting, Ulysses met two men who would play important roles in his career. Congressman Elihu B. Washburne was impressed with Ulysses's experience in the Mexican War. "Captain," he said, "we need just such men as you—men of military education and experience." Washburne became a much-needed political friend in Washington. The other was John Rawlins, a prominent Galena lawyer. He would later serve on Ulysses's staff as a confidante and guardian of his reputation. Rawlins fiercely hated alcohol and was said to keep Ulysses's penchant for it under strict control. He also provided a counterpoint to the calm and collected Ulysses. Rawlins was noted for his temper, expressed in curses so eloquently that Hamlin Garland said, "He could swear in polysyllabic words and in iambic pentameter verse."

Colonel Grant of Illinois

Ulysses declined the captaincy of the Galena company he helped raise. He went to Springfield to serve on Governor Richard Yates's staff. He

White Haven in about 1860. The photograph is from an original carte de visite at the Ulysses S. Grant National Historic Site. *National Park Service.*

inventoried and inspected the weapons in the state arsenal. Yates tapped him to muster in several volunteer regiments around the state. He first traveled to Mattoon to muster in the regiment from Illinois's Seventh Congressional District. His next stop was Belleville across the river from St. Louis, but he was not needed there until May 11. He decided to look in on the old gentleman living at Wish-ton-wish. The Colonel was having financial troubles yet again. He couldn't pay Harry Boggs the money he borrowed. Eventually, Boggs foreclosed on the White Haven estate in September. Fortunately, the place remained in the family when John Dent bought it for $4,226.92.

Although a slave state, Missouri was not prepared to secede from the Union even if Abraham Lincoln won the presidential election of 1860. In the election, Lincoln won only 10 percent of the Missouri vote—mostly from St. Louis, where there was a substantial German immigrant population that was strongly antislavery. Democrat Stephen Douglas and Constitutional Unionist John C. Bell each received 35 percent of the vote; John C. Breckinridge (considered the proslavery candidate) received only 19 percent. Even in the Missouri River counties of Little Dixie, where most of Missouri's slaves and a number of wealthy slave owners lived, Bell did better than Breckinridge.

Missouri did, however, elect Claiborne Fox Jackson—a former Border Ruffian—as governor. Jackson favored secession and secretly took steps to bring Missouri into the Confederate States of America. Jackson coveted the U.S. Arsenal at St. Louis. The arsenal held 60,000 muskets, 90,000 pounds of powder, 1.5 million ball cartridges, 40 cannons and machinery to manufacture weapons. Much of Missouri's early military and political maneuvering centered on gaining control of the arsenal's weapons and ammunition.

Frank Blair Jr., a U.S. congressman and brother of Lincoln's postmaster general, sought to hold the arsenal for the Union. He organized the Home Guards, mostly German American immigrants in St. Louis, to counter secessionist Minute Men. He also successfully sought to have Captain Nathaniel Lyon, a staunch abolitionist, transferred to St. Louis to take command of the arsenal.

In the meantime, Jackson sought and received from the legislature a call for a convention to consider secession on March 4. To Jackson's surprise and dismay, the convention voted overwhelmingly against secession. Missouri wanted to stay in the Union, keep slavery and avoid war. Nonetheless, war came on April 12, 1861. Governor Jackson condemned Lincoln's call for seventy-five thousand volunteers as "illegal, unconstitutional and revolutionary…inhuman and diabolical." Blair mustered his Home Guards into Federal service, and Lyon had those men available to him as well as the regulars stationed at the arsenal.

Governor Jackson ordered the commander of the Missouri Militia, Ulysses's friend and co-sponsor of his failed application for county engineer Daniel Frost, to gather a force near St. Louis for "training." Frost assembled nine hundred men at "Camp Jackson" in Lindell's Grove (now the site of St. Louis University, then outside of the city). Lyon suspected, with good reason, that Jackson and Frost intended to take the arsenal.

On the night of May 9, Ulysses and the Colonel had a long and contentious discussion about the political and military situation. On the morning of May 10, Ulysses wrote to Julia as her father sat in the room, "absorbed in his paper." Ulysses was perturbed that Julia's brother John was considering joining a secession force. He believed that would be a mistake, and John would be better off "to keep cool and claim to have always been for the Union." (John did not join the Confederate army.) As for her father, he "says he is for the Union but is opposed to having an army to sustain it. He would have a secession force march where they please uninterupted and is really what I would call a secessionest." Ulysses noted, "There are two armies now occupying the city, hostile to each other, and I fear there is great danger of a conflict which, if commenced must terminate in great blood shed and destruction of property without advancing the cause of either party." Ulysses went to the city to mail the letter and added a postscript that he saw four thousand men "marching out to the secession encampment to break it up. I very much fear bloodshed."

Colonel Frederick Dent Sr., circa 1860. *Library of Congress.*

Ulysses's fears were realized. Lyon surrounded Camp Jackson and demanded its surrender. Knowing he could not defend against such an overwhelming force, Frost gave up without a fight. But while Lyon's troops were marching the prisoners to town, someone in the crowd of civilians watching the procession fired at the German forces. The Federals returned the fire. Before the melee was over, twenty-eight persons had been killed. Lyon took the prisoners to the arsenal, where they were paroled.

Ulysses disapproved of the political scramble among men seeking to become regimental commanders. As an experienced soldier, he did not want to serve under a green colonel who didn't know the first thing about the military. Yet he wanted to serve. Looking for an appropriate position, Ulysses wrote to the army adjutant general:

> *SIR—Having served for fifteen years in the regular army, including four years at West Point, and feeling it the duty of every one who has been educated at the Government expense to offer their services in support of the Government, I have the honor, very respectfully, to tender my services, until the close of the war, in such capacity as may be offered. I would say, in view of my present age and length of service, I feel myself competent to command a regiment, if the President, in his judgment, should see fit to intrust one to me.*

He felt bold in suggesting a colonelcy, doubting whether he would be up to the task. But he saw some of the men given those positions in Illinois and figured he could do at least as well. Ulysses received no response to his offer from the adjutant general. The letter was apparently lost, only to be found after the war and after he had proved himself worthy of commanding far more than a regiment.

After mustering in the Illinois regiments, Ulysses received permission to go to Covington to visit his family. George McClellan, the newly appointed major general of Ohio troops, had his headquarters in Cincinnati across the Ohio River from Covington. Ulysses decided to seek a position on McClellan's staff but to no avail. He spent two days at McClellan's office, cooling his heels. The general was either "away" or too busy to see an old army comrade. Ulysses was disgusted. He later wrote: "I was older, had ranked him in the army, and could not hang around his headquarters watching men with their quills behind their ears."

One Saturday evening, while Ulysses was visiting his family in Kentucky, Julia had the same dream three times. In that dream, she received an unusual package containing a ring of her mother's that Julia believed should have come to her upon Ellen's death. However, her sister Nell had claimed it. When she opened the package and unwrapped the ring, it "flashed out bright stars on the surrounding paper." From how many times she dreamed it, Julie was certain it meant Nell would realize her mistake and return the ring within the week. She was so sure she wrote to her sister Emma about it.

Ulysses had asked Julia to open and forward any important mail he received while he was gone. He received a letter later that week, and she opened it. Julia describes the experience in her *Memoirs*:

> *I found it contained a sheet of vellum, the face of which was entirely covered with tissue paper, and as I raised my hand to draw down the tissue covering, I exposed to view the great seal of the State of Illinois, which is spangled over with stars; just as in my dream, the ring flashed out its starry light. The letter contained the commission of U.S. Grant as colonel of the 21st Illinois Volunteer Infantry.*

This dream of stars flashing from the ring brought to mind a prophecy made by her mother the summer before she died. Ulysses, Colonel Dent and a group of men were discussing the hot topic of slavery or no slavery, secession or Union, after lunch. Julia and Nell had gone upstairs to rest. Ellen had stayed down and listened to the men for some time before joining her daughters. Ellen pointed a finger, wearing the diamond ring Julia had dreamed about, at the girls and said,

> *I want to make a prophecy this Sunday afternoon.... That little man will fill the highest place in this government. His light is now hid under a bushel, but circumstance will occur, and at no distant day when his worth and wisdom will be shown and appreciated.... He is a great stateman. You will all live to see it, but I will not.... I mean Captain Grant. I have been sitting on the piazza for the last half hour listening to those men talking without the least enlightenment on this important subject, until Captain Grant, in a few sentences, made the subject so clear and our duty so plain that I pronounce him a statesman and a philosopher.*

Julia interpreted the dream about the ring as a message from her mother, reminding her of the prophecy and the great things to come for her husband.

The commission was better news than being a staff officer under McClellan. In the letter, Governor Yates appointed Ulysses colonel of the Twenty-First Illinois Infantry, the regiment he mustered in at Mattoon.

Ulysses decided it would be best for Julia to remain in Galena. Colonel Dent's politics and feelings about Grant's joining the Union army caused a wide breach between them. Dent believed his son-in-law could receive a high rank if he joined the Confederate forces. Letters from St. Louis and other Southern relatives were coming at the Grants fast and furiously, tasking them for their stand with the Union. One of Ulysses's aunts, Rachel Tompkins, a Virginian and ardent secessionist, wrote, "If you are with the accursed Lincolnites, the ties of consanguinity shall be forever severed." It is in Julia's favor that she did not write off her Southern relatives. Her diplomacy proved to be a valuable gift in keeping their relationships not close but salvageable. Even so, Ulysses did not want Julia and the children exposed to the negative feelings directed at him and, by extension, them.

The Twenty-First Illinois Infantry Regiment

The Twenty-First Illinois was a troubled unit. Abram Songer, a lieutenant in Company G, recalled: "To say we were a green, awkward set of men would be stating it in a mild form. All were comparatively young men, and not an officer or man that knew anything about drill or army life." Part of the problem was its commander. Simon Goode had the appearance of a military man but had little knowledge of war. He carried a Bowie knife and wore three revolvers on his belt. Goode quoted Napoleon and boasted of his exploits during William Walker's filibustering campaign in Nicaragua, but as a disciplinarian he was far too soft on the men. Songer complained,

> *He was always ready to forgive anyone gilty of bad conduct. Make him a short speech, tell him he was going to make a brave soldier and then send him to camp, so that all a man had to do was to request an interview with the Col and then be sent to his quarters, which was all a man wanted who was in violation of orders.*

When it was time for the regiment to convert from state militia to a three-year Federal volunteer regiment, the officers asked for a meeting with Governor Yates. Songer reported:

> *The most of the men were ready to go in for three years, but the question* [was how] *to get rid of the man we had elected Colonel. We felt like that* [it] *would not do*[,] *for Good was not fit to command even a Company. The Governer Richard Yates was notified of the condition of things and called the officers to meet him at his office. We obeyed the call, and explained the condition of things to him and told what we were willing to do. That we would enlist for three years if we could get a competent Colonel to command us. His instructions were to return to camp and keep as many of the men together as we could, and he would see what he could do for us.*

Colonel Goode did not receive news of his relief by the newly appointed Colonel Grant well. Samuel Broughton acted as an orderly at headquarters when Goode was notified of his removal. Goode "stormed and raved like a mad man. Swore he would take a musket and follow his regiment and see that his boys were not imposed on. But he thought better of it after he became cool." Broughton saw Goode three years later—after Ulysses was promoted to lieutenant general and made commander of all Union armies. Goode told Broughton that if the officers of the Twenty-First Infantry had not forced him out, he would "have then been filling Grant's position."

Ulysses was pleased with his officers. The company officers were anxious to do well at their duties. As for his lieutenant colonel and major, he commented in a letter to Julia that "I have two men that I think a great deal of but I can never have a game of Eucre with them. One is a preacher and the other a member of Church. For the Field officers of my regt. the 21st Ill. Volunteers one pint of liquor will do to the end of the war."

When Ulysses took over, he imposed the order Goode failed to implement. Not everyone succumbed to Ulysses's strict discipline. Broughton tells of the soldier nicknamed "Mexico." As he recalled:

> *That man would have whiskey. Grant would tie him to a tree every night and keep a guard over him in daytime. On a march Grant would make him carry two guns with a guard over him, but he would get whiskey somehow, and when he came in to camp one night with both gun barrels full he gave it up as a bad job. One day his gun went off, accidentally, he claimed; and the bullet whistled close to Grant's ear. He arrested him for it, but as we had no military prisons then he gave him a furlough, promising to renew it when it expired. That was the last of Mexico. Grant kept his furlough renewed.*

On July 3, the regiment was ordered to Quincy, Illinois. A railroad went directly to Quincy, but Colonel Grant thought it would be beneficial for the regiment's discipline to march there. Songer agreed.

> *I think his idea was a good one for they were at that time a rather unrooley set of men. And he went at it in earnest and accomplished in a short time to perfection as it soon became evident that they were not soldiering under Col Good, and he disciplined the officers as well as the men. I don't think there was an officer but what really feared him, and if they did not they shure respected him. The talk in the regiment then that as Grant was a graduate of West Point, that if the war lasted very long he would get a Brigadier Commission, that was our idea at that time, and little did we think of him ever being promoted as he was later.*

The march was a trying one for the new recruits. Allen Patton wrote from their camp at Naples on the Illinois River that they had marched fifty-five miles in three and a half days, at a rate of about sixteen miles per day.

> [E]*very evening about one third of the regiment is just completely fagged out. I have stood it fine so far and am all sound, with the exception of large blisters under each big toe. All the rest of our mess have taken a turn of giving out or getting sick. They are nearly all well now however. Tye is a little sick and Bill Dills is very sick. Bill was taken sick last night and is*

very sick this morning. He is taking medicine and we think will be able to proceed tomorrow. The other four of us are getting along fine.

Ulysses's son Fred accompanied the regiment on its march. Ulysses reported to Julia that the soldiers called Fred "Colonel" and "he seems quite a favorite." While camped at Naples, the regiment received new orders directing it to Ironton, Missouri. They waited four or five days for a steamer, but it was grounded downriver. Then, Ulysses received word that a regiment was surrounded somewhere west of Hannibal, and he was ordered "to proceed with all dispatch to their relief."

The regiment boarded a train that took them to Quincy after all. Ulysses sent Fred home, writing to Julia, "He did not want to go atall and I felt lothe at sending him but now that we are in the enemies country....I thought you would be alarmed if he was with me. Fred. is a good boy and behaved very manly." Julia replied that she thought Fred should stay with Ulysses, even though he was only eleven years old. After all, Alexander the Great was Fred's age when he went with his father on campaign.

The Twenty-First moved out along the Hannibal & St. Joseph Railroad to make contact with the enemy. In his *Personal Memoirs*, Ulysses confessed to feeling some apprehension as they approached what would be his regiment's first action, but after crossing the Mississippi River, he was relieved to find that "the men of the besieged regiment came straggling into town. I am inclined to think both sides got frightened and ran away."

The Twenty-First moved to Palmyra and from there to the railroad bridge over the Salt River, where it remained for about two weeks as the bridge was replaced. Then, Ulysses was ordered to attack Rebel troops led by Colonel Thomas Harris.

The regiment took several days to collect supplies and wagons and then headed toward Florida, Missouri (Samuel Clemens's birthplace). Grant's account of what happened next is justly famous:

While preparations for the move were going on I felt quite comfortable; but when we got on the road and found every house deserted I was anything but easy....The hills on either side of the creek extend to a considerable height, possibly more than a hundred feet. As we approached the brow of the hill from which it was expected we could see Harris' camp, and possibly find his men ready formed to meet us, my heart kept getting higher and higher until it felt to me as though it was in my throat. I would have given anything then to have been back in Illinois, but I had not the moral

> *courage to halt and consider what to do; I kept right on. When we reached a point from which the valley below was in full view I halted. The place where Harris had been encamped a few days before was still there and the marks of a recent encampment were plainly visible, but the troops were gone. My heart resumed its place. It occurred to me at once that Harris had been as much afraid of me as I had been of him. This was a view of the question I had never taken before; but it was one I never forgot afterwards. From that event to the close of the war, I never experienced trepidation upon confronting an enemy, though I always felt more or less anxiety. I never forgot that he had as much reason to fear my forces as I had his. The lesson was valuable.*

The regiment moved on to Mexico, Missouri, where it remained encamped on the northwest edge of town for a couple of weeks. Ulysses probably visited Graceland, a beautiful mansion owned by John P. Clark, but his headquarters were in a tent next to his men's.

The Twenty-First Illinois had engaged in no more than company drills up to its arrival in Mexico. Ulysses, who had last participated in battalion drills before the Mexican War, had never been trained in the latest infantry formations and movements as embodied in *Hardee's Rifle and Light Infantry Tactics* (the standard infantry manual translated from the French). As many officers did with their first commands, Ulysses sat down with the book the night before to study the first lesson, intending to incorporate new movements each day after a night's homework. But the first time he started to drill the Twenty-First in the fields outside Mexico, he realized that the maneuvers were too cumbersome. They were nothing more than common sense—the "new" tactics were the old tactics, except that instead of halting before each change of direction or formation, the troops just executed the changes while in motion. Ulysses thought neither the officers nor the men had any idea that he had never studied Hardee.

Grant Climbs the Promotion Ladder

While in Mexico, Ulysses learned from a St. Louis newspaper that President Lincoln had asked the Illinois congressional delegation for recommendations for promotion to brigadier general and that they had named Ulysses first in a list of seven. Ulysses wrote that the next day's paper announced that he and three others had been nominated, and they were confirmed shortly afterward. He thanked Congressman Washburne for his influence in obtaining the promotion: "I think I see your hand in it and admit that I had no personal claims for your kind office in the matter."

The new brigadier general first went to take command at Ironton in Southeast Missouri. On the way, he stopped in St. Louis. Ulysses visited his old business partner, Harry Boggs. It did not go well. He wrote to Julia that Boggs

> *cursed and went on like a Madman. Told me that I would never be welcom in his hous; that the people of Illinois* [w]*ere a poor misserable set of Black Republicans, Abolition paupers that had to invade their state to get something to eat. Good joke that on something to eat. Harry is such a pittiful insignificant fellow that I could not get mad at him and told him so where upon he set the Army of Flanders far in the shade with his profanity.*

At Ironton, Ulysses formally received his star. He prepared to attack Confederate forces at Greenville under General William J. Hardee (the author whose *Tactics* Ulysses put aside after one night's study). But he turned command over to Brigadier General Benjamin Prentiss, and the attack did not come off.

Brigadier General Ulysses S. Grant, taken while he was in command at Cairo, Illinois, in 1861. *From Francis T. Miller,* The Photographic History of the Civil War in Ten Volumes: Volume One *(1911).*

Ulysses next went to take command at Jefferson City, where chaos reigned because of Department Commander John C. Frémont's lax recruitment policies. Before any of that could be straightened out, he was sent back to Southeast Missouri to go after Missouri State Guard General M. Jeff Thompson. However, a dispute arose between Ulysses and General Prentiss over who was the senior officer, a common type of pettiness seen throughout the war. Ulysses dismissed it as a "little difficulty of an unpleasant nature he refusing to obey my orders, but it is to be hoped that he will [see] his error and not sacrifice the interest of the cause to his ambition to be Senior Brigadier General of Illinois as he contends he is." The expedition fizzled out when Prentiss quit in a snit and left for St. Louis.

Ulysses went to Cairo, Illinois, to assume command of Southern Illinois and Southeast Missouri. Shortly after arriving at his new headquarters, Ulysses got wind of a Confederate attempt to seize Paducah, Kentucky, an important town on the Ohio River at the mouth of the Tennessee River. He immediately occupied Paducah, to the dismay of many of its citizens, who were preparing to receive the Southern troops.

The General's First Battle

Ulysses's men at Cairo were getting restless. They enlisted to fight the Confederate army but hadn't fought anyone yet. When he received orders to send troops down the Mississippi to prevent the Rebels from sending troops from Columbus to the Missouri side, he had his chance to show his green regiments what war was like. He couldn't capture Columbus. It was occupied by 17,000 men, commanded by Leonidas Polk. They sat behind formidable fortifications on the 150-foot bluffs armed with 140 heavy cannon. But he could go after a much smaller force of about 2,500 men across the river at Belmont.

On the evening of November 6, Ulysses boarded about three thousand men aboard six steamboats. The force proceeded downstream to a few miles above Belmont, accompanied by two timberclad gunboats (prewar steamboats protected by five-inch oak planks instead of iron). The next morning, the force dropped down to Lucas Bend, a short distance from Belmont, where the expedition was protected from the Columbus batteries by a sharp curve in the river. The gunboats made a demonstration against the fort at Columbus while Ulysses and his men went ashore.

Ulysses formed his men into a battle line and sent skirmishers out front. They came upon the Confederate forces at about 9:00 a.m. The firefight lasted until noon. The Rebels abandoned their camp and huddled under the riverbank. At this point, Ulysses lost control of his men. They began celebrating their victory by looting the enemy's camp to the sound of bands playing patriotic music. Officers ostentatiously proclaimed victory. Illinois politician and General John McClernand made a particularly bombastic "spread-eagle speech."

Battle of Belmont. *From* Frank Leslie's Illustrated Newspaper, *Library of Congress.*

But the battle wasn't over. General Frank Cheatham boarded five regiments at Columbus and made the short trip across the river. Ulysses and his men were too busy celebrating to notice until it was too late. The men panicked. Ulysses calmly ordered troops to burn the camp and tried to rally them. They were beyond rallying, however, and made for the boats at Lucas Bend and safety. The last man to make it to the boats was Ulysses Grant. He gingerly rode his horse down a steep bank (the river was very low) and over a single plank to the steamboat's prow. Exhausted, Ulysses threw himself on the sofa in the captain's cabin. He decided to check on the status of his troops and the boats. At just that moment, "a musket ball entered that room, struck the head of the sofa, passed through it and lodged in the foot."

Ulysses regarded the Battle of Belmont as a great victory, and in November 1861, perhaps it passed for that in the wake of disasters at Bull Run, Wilson's Creek and Lexington. It had no lasting strategic significance. Belmont was essentially a raid that began well and ended badly. It would not be long before Ulysses had many more important successes.

Missouri saw over one thousand military engagements during the Civil War—the third most after Virginia and Tennessee. The Battle of Belmont was the only one Ulysses fought in the state that had been his and Julia's home.

12

"UNCLE SAM" GRANT BECOMES "UNCONDITIONAL SURRENDER" GRANT

When Ulysses moved his headquarters to Cairo, Illinois, he asked Julia to join him and bring the children. It was his request to include the children that made her hesitate. It was difficult to travel with four children in tow. She was agitated during the preparations and, at one point, went upstairs to rest and calm herself. Here, she had another vision. "I distinctly saw Ulys a few rods from me. I only saw his head and shoulders, only about as high as if he were on horseback. He looked at me so earnestly, and I thought, so reproachfully that I started up and said 'Ulys!'" Her friend in the next room asked if she was all right, and Julia replied that she was only a bit nervous, but she'd soon see her husband. She and the children started out that evening. She had news of the Battle of Belmont before leaving.

Ulysses met the family at the train when they arrived in Cairo, and Julia told him of her vision. He asked her when she had it. She told him, and Ulysses responded in wonderment that was at the end of the Battle of Belmont: "Just about that time I was on horseback and in great peril, and I thought of you and the children, and what would become of you if I were lost. I was thinking of you, my dear Julia, and very earnestly too."

Julia and the children stayed in Cairo until the end of November, when she went to St. Louis. She found "home" a changed and uncomfortable place. Her father, of course, continued to moan and groan about Ulysses's allegiance to the Union; many of her friends were openly and solidly Southern, and old military friends were Confederate officers. She knew how it felt to be the enemy.

Julia and the children returned to Cairo in December.

FORT HENRY AND FORT DONELSON

Ulysses prepared for yet another expedition against Rebel forces—this one of far more strategic importance than the raid on Belmont. Conferring with Flag Officer Andrew Foote, in charge of the so-called Brown Navy gunboats on the Ohio River, they plotted a campaign up the twin rivers of the Tennessee and Cumberland. On January 23, Ulysses left for St. Louis to present the plan to the new departmental commander, General Henry W. Halleck. In his *Personal Memoirs*, Ulysses said Halleck received him with "little cordiality." Presumably, the stiff and proud Halleck thought that it was impertinent for a district commander to propose such a major movement to a department commander. Upon his return to Cairo, Ulysses telegraphed Halleck that "if permitted, I could take and hold Fort Henry on the Tennessee." Halleck, perhaps satisfied that he could claim credit for any victories and avoid blame for any defeat, immediately gave Grant and Foote the go-ahead.

On February 6, 1862, Fort Henry fell to the combined forces of Ulysses's army and Flag Officer Foote's gunboats. Fort Donelson on the Cumberland River fell to Union forces within ten days. Confederate General Simon Buckner—the same man who bailed Ulysses out in New York City on his return from California in 1854—sought terms for surrender. Ulysses responded with the famous letter that gave him his newest and most durable nickname:

Hd Qrs, Army in the. Field
Camp near Donelson, Feb.y 16th 1862

GEN. S.B. BUCKNER,
CONFED. ARMY,

SIR;

Yours of this date proposing Armistice, and appointment of commissioners, to settle terms of capitulation is just received. No terms except an unconditional and immediate surrender can be accepted.

I propose to move immediately upon your works.

I am sir; very respectfully
your obt. servt.
U.S. GRANT
Brig. Gen.

"Uncle Sam" Grant, a previously obscure officer in the U.S. Army who left the service for an equally obscure civilian life, became overnight a national sensation as "Unconditional Surrender" Grant. From February 1862 to April 1865, Ulysses would lead the Union armies to ultimate victory in the Civil War.

Adventures of the General's Wife

Although the North originally went to war to restore the Union, by late 1862 it had become clear that to win the war, it had to free slaves. Despite her husband's growing prominence in prosecuting the war and his evolution from "practical liberator" to moral emancipator, Julia kept the enslaved persons—Eliza, Dan, Jules and John—her father had given her. Jules traveled with her as maid and nurse when Julia was in states where slavery was still legal, much to the chagrin of Ulysses. Julia never expressed any remorse for holding humans as property. And when the enslaved began to be restless with the approach of Union victory that would mean freedom for them, Julia was sure it meant only they were upset because they'd lose all the comforts provided by their enslavers. Jules finally left for Ohio and freedom in January 1864 while the family was at Louisville.

Julia's main role during the Civil War was supporting her husband. He always wanted her physical presence when he felt she would be safe in camp. When they were apart, Ulysses counted on her letters and Julia's taking care of business, such as managing their finances, property and the children's education. Her attention to these details of everyday life let him focus on his military role as leader of the Union army without distractions.

When Julia was in Southern locations with Ulysses, she sometimes found herself in situations with loyal Southern women. They were friendly, included her at times and insisted she must be a Southerner herself. Like many Missourians, Julia refuted their claim, insisting she was a Westerner.

Julia remained in Cairo with Ulysses until the end of January 1862, when she went to Covington. In the spring of 1862, she and the four children met Ulysses in Shiloh. Julia returned to Covington and then came to Jackson, Mississippi, in October of that year. Later, she was with her husband in Nashville. Julia always came when Ulysses requested and made do with whatever arrangements were available—from house to tent, to hotel to cabin. She felt it was good for him to have his family near, and as a result, both wife and children developed a public persona, recognizable and in danger of being kidnapped by Confederates.

Emma, Julia's sister, wrote about a close call involving Julia's and Ulysses's son Fred. He had come to Caseyville, Kentucky, to visit his aunt and her husband. Many guerrillas roamed the area, and at times, despite the risk, Fred and Mr. Casey, his uncle, would ride into town.

One morning, when they were gone, a man dressed in a worn Confederate uniform rode up and asked Emma for a drink of water, and she gave him one. As he drank, he said, "Fred Grant is your visitor, isn't he?

Emma felt cold with dread. "No, he's not here," she said.

"Is that so?" He smiled at her.

Again, she insisted he'd gone.

He mumbled to himself, mounted his horse, bowed to Emma and rode off.

Emma quickly sent one of her enslaved to find Fred and Mr. Casey, with a message to put Fred on a boat and send him to Cairo as soon as possible. She also suggested telling one of the gunboats guarding the river what had happened and having them keep an eye on the lad. But the story wasn't over.

Later, a man rode up to the house on a tired and thirsty horse. Emma gave them both water.

"You have a boy here, have you not?"

"No, the boy has gone," Emma said.

With another smile as the man had earlier, her present "guest" said, "Well, I suppose a hint to the wise is sufficient." And he was gone.

That afternoon, a squad of eight "hard-riding, grim-looking, and tattered cavalrymen approached the Caseys' gate." One of them came to the porch. "Is this Mr. Casey's?" he asked politely.

Emma said it was.

"Isn't there a boy visiting here?"

"No, he has gone back to his mother."

"Are you sure?"

"Yes, and I think there is likely to be some gunboats coming up the river very shortly looking for someone. Perhaps you gentlemen will be interested in seeing them."

The man returned to his squad; they talked among themselves, waved their hats to Emma and rode away.

Emma was sure they were up to no good and knew that if they'd taken the boy, it would have been a hard blow at Ulysses.

In December 1862, Confederate cavalry raided the Union supply base at Holly Springs, Mississippi, where Julia, her son Jesse and Jules were staying

Fortunately, the day before the raid, they joined Ulysses at his headquarters in Oxford. The raiders took Julia's horses and burned her carriage. A Southern lady protected Julia's personal property. The lady was later rewarded by Julia's intercession on her behalf when that lady's husband was taken prisoner. Ulysses also issued an order that the woman's house was not to be destroyed or raided.

Throughout the war, Julia was concerned about Ulysses's reputation. She was quick to deny rumors of his drinking. She believed he was "honest in all his interactions and right in all his decisions." This unshakeable belief in him gave Ulysses the confidence he needed to succeed.

Julia also became a savvy businesswoman during those years, thanks to Ulysses's tutelage. Ulysses purchased White Haven from John Dent in 1864. Julia dealt with the recalcitrant Joseph White at Hardscrabble and later oversaw leases on portions of White Haven.

Julia nursed sick and injured soldiers in the camps for a time but stopped when Ulysses asked her to do so. He didn't want her exposed to that part of the war. She tried not to listen to all the requests for her intercession with her husband, but sometimes it was difficult.

VICKSBURG

One of Julia's most memorable glimpses of the war was at Vicksburg. Julia and the children had come down from Memphis. She dined on board the *Henry von Phul* with other officers and their wives, and when it was dark, they moved downriver to watch boats attempt to get past the batteries at Vicksburg. Julia described the running of the blockade in her *Memoirs*:

> *All was going well when a red glare flashed up from the Vicksburg shore and the flotilla of gunboats and transports and our own boats was made plainly visible. Indeed, it was a grand sight; the long stretch of river at the end of which was the blazing house illuminating it. How vividly the picture is photographed on my mind; the grand roar of the cannon rests in my memory. The batteries of Vicksburg poured shot and shell on the heads of the devoted little fleet, but Porter was there—thank Heaven!—to return broadside for broadside. The air was full of sulphurous smoke. The batteries were passed, and we rested here awaiting the report of casualties, and were happy to learn there had been no loss of life, although some few*

> *were wounded.…The smoke cleared away, the stars looked down tenderly on Union and Rebel alike, and the katydids and the frogs began again their summer songs.*

Julia watched with her shawl wrapped tight around her, seemingly unafraid and reaching out for Ulysses when shells exploded. The shelling frightened son Jesse, and Ulysses sent him below deck.

Fred had been begging to leave school and accompany his father. He joined him at the campaign at Vicksburg. From that point on, he slept in his father's tent and shared the soldiers' mess. They were sometimes exposed to enemy fire as they examined the siege lines together, to the dismay of Ulysses's aides. Fred was wounded slightly on one of the inspections, but his father proudly said, "Fred never knew what it was to be afraid." Fred remembered it a bit differently, commenting after a visit to a hospital where the wounded lay bleeding and mangled: "Here were scenes so terrible that I became faint, and making my way to a tree, sat down, the most woebegone twelve-year-old lad in America."

Julia and the other children returned to St. Louis and Wish-ton-wish for an uncomfortable summer. All her neighbors were Southern and could not believe Julia was not. When she denied it, they would say, "It is right for you to say you are Union, Julia, but we know better.…It is not in human nature

Admiral Porter running the blockade at Vicksburg. *Library of Congress.*

for you to be anything but Southern." Her friends baited Julia by speaking of sending mail to the South, and Julia would threaten it was her duty to tell the authorities. The women would smile and insist she would not because of her upbringing: "An oath would not be more binding than the sanctity of your roof." She didn't tell.

Her father constantly argued with Julia about the Constitution. Julia was perplexed about all the talk of the document. She said she had never seen it and wouldn't even know where to look for it. Finally, she suggested that since the present Constitution was so confusing, why not make a new one?

Young Jesse recalled a very telling incident during this visit about the Civil War conditions in Missouri. He and his cousin went riding, only the two of them. When they returned to Wish-ton-wish, no one was there. The boys knew there were alarms out for guerrilla raids in the neighborhood and feared the home had been raided and their family kidnapped. They rode as fast as their ponies would carry them into St. Louis, right up the marble steps to the Southern Hotel and straight through to the office where Jesse knew he'd be recognized. His mother and the rest of the family were safe and sound. Julia had left a note the boys missed, and the enslaved servants had fled to White Haven, having heard of raiders. Unfortunately, Jesse's pony refused to descend the marble steps it had so nimbly ascended and had to be carried down by one of the enslaved hotel employees.

Despite all the negativity Julia faced during her visit, she and the children enjoyed the country.

One day in early July, there was a hail of artillery fire. Julia said it must mean that Vicksburg had surrendered. Soon, she was proven right, and she received an invitation to go into the city to attend a parade to honor her husband's victory. It was several days before the victory was affirmed, and Julia and the children prepared to return to Ulysses in Vicksburg.

Before she left, her son Fred arrived in St. Louis ill. Fred and Buck stayed behind with their grandfather while she returned to Ulysses. Not long after, she brought Nellie to school in St. Louis and brought Jesse with her.

Julia traveled back and forth throughout the South as Grant moved his army. While she was in Nashville, again at Ulysses's request, she received notice that her son Fred was gravely ill in St. Louis. A major from Ulysses's staff accompanied her and Jesse, and when they arrived at East St. Louis, they found the river was frozen over. It was possible to cross by omnibus, but Julia refused, worrying it might break through the ice. She, Jesse and the major walked nearly a mile across the ice at midnight.

Fred was sick with camp dysentery and typhoid. He continued to grow more ill, and Ulysses was sent for. A second doctor came in and suggested a change in medicine. The medicine worked, Fred recovered and the family returned to Nashville.

A Constant and Needed Companion

Julia visited Washington, D.C., with her husband after he was promoted to lieutenant general and commander of all the Union armies. She then traveled to the Sanitary Fair and visited friends in New York. Julia left the city for St. Louis to check on her three oldest children, who were in school there and under the care of her cousin, Louisa Boggs.

St. Louis was also the site of a sanitary fair to raise money for supplies for the Union troops. The Western Sanitary Commission's Fair opened on May 17, 1864, and closed in June. There was an admission fee and booths with articles for purchase, raffles and activities. Daughter Nellie had a "starring" role in the fair, portraying the old woman in the shoe who had so many children she didn't know what to do. Julia recalled in her *Memoirs* that "Nellie was delighted with her metamorphosis, seated as she was in a mammoth black pasteboard shoe filled with beautiful dolls of all sizes. Nellie wore over her pretty curls a wide, ruffled cap and a pair of huge spectacles across her pretty, rosy, dimpled face." The dolls could be purchased for fifty cents, accompanied by a photo of Nellie. The children were very excited by their adventures at the fair and brought Julia an array of small gifts they purchased or won there, including a doll from Nellie's old shoe.

Nellie Grant as the old lady who lived in a shoe at the Mississippi Valley Sanitary Fair, St. Louis, May–June 1864. *National Park Service.*

Eventually, Ulysses called for Julia to return to the East, specifically to Philadelphia, because he felt the family would be safe there. She and the children traveled there, but Julia couldn't find suitable accommodation, so they ended up in Burlington, New Jersey, where the children attended school. Julia and Ulysses visited each other, sometimes Julia in D.C. and sometimes Ulysses in New Jersey, although he was often distracted by military business.

On one visit to Washington, Ulysses requested Jesse stay behind with him. Julia was reluctant to leave their "baby." They asked Jesse what he wished to do, and he said if his mamma agreed, he'd stay behind. The family moved along to the steamer, unloading Jesse's baggage, when the boy threw himself to the floor and claimed he was very hurt and must go along with his mamma. Fred was the one disappointed. He wanted very much to be with his father in the middle of the war.

Fred was allowed to spend the Christmas holidays with his father. One of his activities was a duck hunt down the James River. He wore his school

Grant family in the 1860s. Photos and portraits made the Grants very visible to and identifiable by the public. *Missouri Historical Society*.

uniform, gray with black trim, and traveled by rowboat, rowed by one of his father's African American bodymen. On the river, a gunboat fired at them and ordered Fred on board, thinking he was a Rebel. It took Fred some time to convince his captors he wasn't a Confederate in his gray uniform but the son of General Grant.

Ulysses and Julia, 1864. *Library of Congress.*

Julia's stay with Ulysses at City Point from June 1864 to April 1865 was one of the longest times she spent with her husband during the war. She was familiar with the peace discussions and met all the key players in the drama. At one point, Ulysses approached her with the idea she might be able to make peace overtures with the Confederates through their wives.

> *"See here, Mrs. Grant, what do you think of this? Ord has been across the lines on a flag of truce and brings a suggestion that terms of peace may be reached through you, and a suggestion of an interchange of social visits between you and Mrs. Longstreet and others when the subject of peace may be discussed, and you ladies may become the mediums of peace." At once, I exclaimed: "Oh! How enchanting, how thrilling! Oh, Ulys, I may go, may I not?" He only smiled at my enthusiasm and said: "No, that would never do."*

Ulysses feared Julia might propose a policy of her devising that Lincoln would not approve. After all, as Julia said, she had always had a desire to have a voice in great affairs. Ulysses, in the chauvinistic manner of the day, finished the discussion by declaring, "The men have fought this war, and the men will finish it." He didn't consider that the women of the day had also been part of the war. Julia was disappointed and certain, even years later, that the idea of her involvement had not originated with her husband but with General Ord.

Above: Ulysses, Julia and Jesse Grant at City Point, Virginia, 1864. *Missouri Historical Society.*

Opposite: Lieutenant General Ulysses S. Grant, commander of the Union armies, at Cold Harbor, Virginia, June 1864. *Library of Congress.*

Julia received notice of the surrender and peace agreement from a telegraph operator who told her she deserved to know the news as soon as anyone, including the president. The rest of her companions knew quickly after, and they all celebrated. On the Monday evening following the news, Julia received word to prepare a late dinner for her husband. She and the other wives waiting with her sang, danced and celebrated until they were exhausted, and their husbands still had not come. Around 4:00 a.m., they retired to rest but stayed dressed. Julia fell asleep but awoke to Ulysses's return the next morning.

Julia and her general sailed into Washington that day to a hero's welcome. Once Julia was settled, Ulysses proceeded to the White House to meet with President Lincoln.

An Invitation Declined

A few days later, Julia wanted nothing more than to return to New Jersey with Ulysses to see the children. He said he had to meet with the president before he could leave, and it might be too late in the day, especially after Lincoln asked to delay the meeting. Still, Julia insisted it must be that day, no matter the time.

At midday, a man dressed in "light colored corduroy coat and trousers and with rather a shabby hat of the same color" appeared at Julia's door. He said, "Mrs. Lincoln sends me, Madam, with her compliments to say she will call for you at exactly eight o'clock to go to the theater." Julia found the messenger discourteous and the "invitation" more of a command. Julia and Mary Todd Lincoln had not hit it off in their few meetings. Julia replied, "You may return with my compliments to Mrs. Lincoln and say that I regret that as General Grant and I intend leaving the city this afternoon, we will not, therefore, be here to accompany the President and Mrs. Lincoln." The man countered that newspapers had already announced the president's and General Grant's attendance at the performance. Julia repeated that they could not attend, and he must deliver her message as given.

After this encounter, Julia felt even more strongly that she and Ulysses must leave Washington that day. She sent a message to her husband, telling him she had refused the theater invitation and that they must leave for home. She sent the same message urging the general to go to New Jersey that evening via three staff officers. Ulysses gave in and sent a note telling

Julia to take Jesse to lunch and have their bags ready, and he would try to join them on the afternoon train to Philadelphia. During the lunch with Jesse and another military wife, four men entered the restaurant and sat near them. Julia thought one of them was the messenger from that morning. Another of the men seemed to listen intently to their conversation, watching them without eating even one bite of his meal, although he had pretended to. She asked her friend to look, and the woman agreed they were "peculiar."

Later that day, on the way to the station, the same man who had stared at Julia and made her so uncomfortable in the restaurant rode by their carriage on a dark horse, turned around and returned, glaring at Ulysses through the carriage window. The look he had on his face made even Ulysses uncomfortable. The rest of the trip was uneventful.

The couple and Jesse stopped for a bite to eat while waiting for the ferry to Burlington, and as soon as he sat down, Ulysses received three telegrams. The president had been assassinated.

The family proceeded home, and then Ulysses left as soon as arrangements could be made to return to Washington.

The next morning, Julia opened a letter to her husband, who asked her to do the same. It said: "General Grant, thank God, as I do, that you still live. It was your life that fell to my lot, and I followed you onto the cars. Your door was locked, and thus you escaped me. Thank God." Once again, Julia's insistence on returning to their home and children affected the life of her Ulysses. Was it another premonition? Or was it, as her sister Emma claimed, another dream? Or was it a wife and mother who simply wanted her family together after a long separation?

13
POSTWAR YEARS

In honor of Ulysses's triumph in the war, the people of Philadelphia presented him with a grand house. Julia found the house perfect in every way, including furnishings. Since she had heard of the gift, Julia had saved her pin money to purchase a silver service, but that, too, was included.

Daughter Nellie asked her mother when they were going home after they moved into the Philadelphia house. Julia informed her they were home and would live in the house forever. Nellie insisted, "No, mamma, no, this is not our home. I have just come from there. Our house is a great, great house (with a struggle to say what it was like) like…like…the picture in my geography of the…the…Capitol in Washington; I know. I was there." Nellie evidently inherited her mother's ability to prophesize via her dreams because she said, "Why of course I was dreaming, for I have been here ever since we came to the party." The party was the reception upon their arrival.

Life in Washington, D.C.

The Grants—meaning Julia, Nellie and Jesse—lived in the Philadelphia house for four years while Grant worked almost nonstop in the War Department in Washington. Sometimes, he would make it home, but he was always called back within twenty-four hours. The older boys were still in school in Burlington, New Jersey. Julia was lonely and unhappy and

Julia, 1865. *Library of Congress.*

finally asked her husband to move them to Washington with him. Ulysses agreed. "It does seem that life is too short for us to live apart." Julia, Nellie and Jesse joined Ulysses in the capital.

Julia found the house Ulysses rented for his family in Georgetown uncomfortable and too expensive. She insisted they find a place of their own. Ulysses immediately thought of a place in the country. He still wanted to raise horses and grow crops. They found nothing appropriate close enough to the city, and properties in the city were too expensive.

Ulysses's brother-in-law Abel Corbin inquired about their living arrangements and offered to sell them a house on hearing what rent they were paying and gave them ten years to pay for it. Julia did some basic math to figure out the finances of the deal. (She improved her math skills greatly while taking care of home finances and family business during the war.) They were paying $2,500 per year in rent in Georgetown. Over the ten years their friend allowed them to pay to buy the house, the sum would equal the cost of the house. Julia presented the plan to her husband: pay $10,000 up front and then spread the remainder plus interest over the next ten years. At first, Ulysses was hesitant but agreed once he saw the house.

The Grants tried to give back their Philadelphia home, as they had promised to live in it and were not going to do so. The committee who had gifted the house refused plus told them to move the furniture into their new home and rent the Philadelphia house.

On the home front, Ulysses's approach with the children was to let them do as they pleased so long as it didn't interfere with their duties. Julia insisted his word was law around the house, but when asked to deal with a child-involved issue, he said, "You must not quarrel with mamma. She knows what is best for you, and you must always obey her."

The family traveled often, and they were greeted by former soldiers, their wives and widows everywhere they went. They were met with great receptions, cheers, bouquets of flowers and clamoring for speeches by the general. Julia was glad to share her husband with the public. As she

Grant's family: Ulysses, Jesse, Buck, Fred, Nellie and Julia, 1867. *National Park Service.*

said, she had long years alone with Lieutenant Grant when they rode together through the woods on their horses.

Julia remembered their four years in Washington between the war and Grant's presidential nomination as "a pleasant memory of dinners, balls, and receptions, of pleasant people who said kind things, and some pleasant visits away from Washington." Would Ulysses describe them likewise?

While Julia was enjoying the social life of Washington, Ulysses was dealing with increasing political troubles in his position as army commander. President Johnson and Radical Republicans clashed over Reconstruction policy. Ulysses was often left in the middle.

Johnson insisted that Ulysses accompany him on what came to be called the "Swing Around the Circle"—a series of speeches in which the president sought to rally the country in opposition to the proposed Fourteenth Amendment, which, among other provisions, explicitly recognized the citizenship of African Americans (overruling the *Dred Scott* decision) by declaring that all persons born or naturalized in the United States were citizens and guaranteeing due process of law and equal protection of the laws for everyone. Although Ulysses supported the Fourteenth Amendment, he reluctantly complied with the president's request out of loyalty to the office, if not the man. But Ulysses finally could take no more, leaving the

"Swing" in St. Louis. He wrote to Julia, "I have never been so tired of anything before as I have been with the political speeches of Mr. Johnson from Washington to this place. I look upon them as a National disgrace." His old friend and former staff officer William Hillyer gave a speech in which he claimed Ulysses supported President Johnson. Ulysses wrote him a blistering letter, saying, "You, nor no man living, is authorized to speak for me in political matters, and I ask [you] to desist in the future. I want every man to vote according to his own judgment, without influence from me."

Flush with money for the first time in his life, and to take a break from the bitter politics of the day, Ulysses decided to make White Haven his dream. He began to reacquire the property sold during the war. In November 1866, he wrote to his father that he had "some six or seven hundred acres of the Dent farm." Even during his presidency, Ulysses gave detailed instructions to the caretakers on what to plant, what structures to tear down (he ordered the cabins that were former homes of the enslaved farmhands torn down in 1867) and what structures to build. Ulysses was particularly anxious to make their former home on the Gravois a horse farm. For that, he needed a substantial barn in which to stable the animals. It was built in 1871. Although

President Grant's farm at White Haven (*upper*) the ruins of Wish-ton-wish (*lower left*) and the horse barn Ulysses directed to be built (*lower right*). Leslie's Illustrated Newspaper, *National Park Service*

moved from its original location to make way for new suburban homes, the barn still stands and serves as the museum for the Ulysses S. Grant National Historic Site.

Not all went well, however. Wish-ton-wish burned down in 1873. While Ulysses had some prize horses, the farm was barely profitable. He closed it down in 1875.

PRESIDENCY

A constant refrain in 1868 was that the Republicans would nominate Grant for the office of president. When Ulysses and Julia returned to Galena, the town gave them yet another house. Asked about running for president, Ulysses joked: "I am not a candidate for any office, but I would like to be mayor of Galena long enough to fix the sidewalks, especially the one reaching to my house." He was met the next day with a banner that read, "GENERAL, THE SIDEWALK IS BUILT."

Julia preferred that Ulysses remain general-in-chief, a military man. When the convention was about to start, Julia asked Ulys if he wanted to be

Left: President Ulysses S. Grant. *Library of Congress*.

Right: Julia Dent Grant, 1876. *Library of Congress*.

president. He replied, "No, but I do not see that I have anything to say about it. The convention…will nominate me; and if I am nominated, I suppose I will be elected." After Julia reminded him of Johnson's troubles in office, Ulysses said, "I do not want to be President. But I feel if I am nominated I must accept as a duty, and I feel, too, that I can give to the widely separated interests and sections of the country more satisfaction than any other man."

Ulysses S. Grant was nominated on the first ballot. That summer, the Fourteenth Amendment was ratified. When Election Day arrived, Ulysses voted the straight Republican ticket, except for one office. He left his vote for president blank. On March 4, 1869, he was sworn in as president of the United States. Ellen Dent's prediction about her son-in-law had come true.

Julia in the White House

At first, Julia refused to leave the Washington home where the family had such a good life. Ulysses announced he'd sold that house. Julia refused to sign the deed, and Ulysses had to cancel the sale. Friends of General William Sherman bought the house for the general to reclaim later, and Julia approved.

Once installed, Julia loved living in the White House. She redecorated and rehabbed the long-neglected residence. Julia spent the first $25,000 that Congress gave to all new presidents on the family quarters and executive offices on the second floor. She found adding updated plumbing and closets to the family's residence essential. During Ulysses's second term, Congress gave them $100,000, and Julia used that to hire professional decorators to redo public rooms.

Sons Fred and Buck were away at school, Fred at West Point and Buck at Harvard, but Jesse and Nellie still lived with Julia and Ulysses. Julia tried sending them to boarding school, but because neither liked it, they returned to the White House. The back lawn was closed off to give the children a place to play and Julia a place to spend time outdoors, although they received criticism for doing it.

As the president's wife, Julia saw herself as a public figure and felt a sense of entitlement in her role. However, she knew anything she did that was publicly acknowledged, positive or negative, would reflect on her husband. Yet, she accepted gifts and privileges without regard to who gave them or whether it might appear a conflict of interest.

The term *first lady* had not come into use, although Julia was referred to by at least one newspaper in Honolulu as the "first lady of the land." Other women in prominent positions were also called this, such as Queen Victoria and the wife of the chief justice of the Supreme Court.

Still, Julia maintained a sense of honor. For example, when asked to contribute a recipe to the Centennial Cookbook, she found herself in a quandary. Julia had no recipes of her own—she had always had servants to cook for her. Julia finally submitted a chicken gumbo recipe but noted that it was a friend's and not of her own making.

FAMILY LIFE

Because Julia was so willing to share her life and that of her children with the public (and had done so since the Civil War), a new concept, the "first family," was established, although not referred to in those terms until much later. The Grants were referred to as the president's family or the White House family.

Once the children had finished their education, they traveled. Fred accompanied General Sherman to Europe, although newspapers sometimes reported that Sherman was accompanying Fred. Buck and Nellie also visited "the Continent," and Jesse went to California.

In 1874, both Nellie and Fred married.

When Algernon Sartoris, an Englishman, asked Ulysses for Nellie's hand, it was a replay of the scenario when Grant asked Colonel Dent for Julia's hand. Ulysses argued his daughter was too young and wouldn't be content living a quiet life in the English countryside. He later said he'd prefer she not marry at all and stay closer to family, but if she had to marry, she should marry an American. Nevertheless, Nellie married Sartoris at the White House in a wedding whose elegance starkly contrasted with her parents' quiet nuptials. Ulysses was silent and sad, with tears on his cheeks during the ceremony. The president couldn't be found when the couple left for their train. He was in Nellie's room, sobbing his heart out.

Fred brought his new bride home soon after, and they made Julia and Ulysses grandparents of a girl named after her great-grandmother. Baby Ellen Dent was christened in the Blue Room of the White House.

Colonel Dent also resided in the White House with his daughter. In one incident, the president was entertaining guests with the Colonel present.

A political question came up, and the old gentleman declared, "I am a Democrat, the same as ever, and don't believe in any other party…and you young fellows cannot bring me over to your new party." As one of those present later recorded, Ulysses smiled, and his "eyes twinkled more than once at his [father-in-law's] harmless and witty observations." Julia often seated her father next to her at meals to keep him from saying something outrageous to one or another of their guests.

The New White House

Besides shining up the inside of the White House, Julia and Ulysses brought other new practices and ideas with them. The couple dined in public restaurants, something the president had not done before. They also made social calls to the homes of friends in the city. Julia's public receptions were open to everyone, including African Americans. Yet none attended. When Julia asked why, she learned the stewards had turned them away. The daytime receptions, both Ulysses's and Julia's, came to be known as less formal and more sociable than those held by prior presidents and their wives. For the first time, the press was given access to the president's wife and the White House. Julia often had press members come in before a big event so the reports would be accurate, although she said that seldom happened.

Julia hired an Italian chef who had worked in grand hotels to prepare meals for their formal and state dinners. Sometimes, the dinners would include twenty-one courses, although Julia made sure they moved along and lasted not more than two hours. She also worked a bit of "china diplomacy." The White House china ordered by Julia was decorated with the state flower of every state in the Union to avoid the appearance of any preference for one state or region over another.

Julia knew the White House from attic to cellar and was also familiar with the staff. She advised them about money and, in times of trouble, helped out.

Ulysses and Julia traveled, although the demands of the presidency often made it difficult. They visited St. Louis almost yearly to see family and friends and check on their properties there. Ulysses still dreamed of raising horses at White Haven after his presidential term ended. However, on April 21, 1873, on a visit to St. Louis, he said, "I shall endeavor in the future to make my visits frequent, although I much doubt I shall ever make my permanent residence here again. I have never lived long enough in one place to form a very close attachment to it, except here and in Washington."

During a visit in 1874 for the Mechanical and Agricultural Fair in St. Louis, Ulysses's horses won several blue ribbons. Rumors abounded that the ribbons were more in honor of the owner than the horse. When Ulysses visited the city with or without Julia, he stayed with friends in their homes on Lucas Place or at the Lindell Hotel, as they had leased White Haven. At least four times, he dined at Robert Campbell's home and on Lucas Place. Grant had appointed Campbell, a friend, as Indian peace commissioner to oversee the distribution of annuities to Native Americans. Visits to St. Louis became rarer as time passed, and in 1884, the Grants lost their last tangible link to St. Louis when they signed over White Haven to Cornelius Vanderbilt in payment for a loan.

Julia's extrasensory powers hadn't left her. On a trip to Chicago in 1871, she had a dream that saved them once again. She dreamed of smoke coming from a large bird and insisted they leave the city immediately. Upon their arrival in Washington, the Grants learned that a great two-day fire had nearly destroyed Chicago.

Julia was publicly acknowledged by friends, the press, the public and Ulysses himself as an asset. They were also straightforward in showing their love and affection freely. They used nicknames for one another: Ulyss or Lyss by Julia, Mrs. G by Ulysses. They spent time alone together, often with Ulysses reading aloud to his wife as her eyesight worsened. They ate breakfast together daily; the president accompanied his wife back to her sitting room, where they chatted again, and then he went to work at his desk. Julia thought nothing of barging in on the president at work to talk about nothing in particular and having to be asked to leave so he could concentrate on important matters. Most unusual for presidents and their wives, Julia and Ulysses shared a bed, always, including in the White House.

Ulysses usually denied his wife's political influence, but sometimes it came into play. Hamilton Fish, Grant's secretary of state, offered to resign after he failed to annex Santa Domingo. Julia Fish was a close friend and confidante of Julia's. Women friends, wives of cabinet and Senate members, often stood with Julia Grant at receptions and, because of her eyesight and her vain refusal to wear glasses, helped her identify the faces of those coming through the line so she could greet them appropriately. Because Mrs. Fish was one of the women Julia relied on for social support, Grant refused her husband's resignation.

Julia noticed that Kate Williams, the wife of Grant's attorney general, suddenly seemed to have much more money to spend on frivolities. This observation gave credence to a claim (later admitted) that her husband, William, had halted a federal case against a New York mercantile house after Kate received a $30,000 bribe.

Although Julia might have influenced minor appointments or ensured certain people had access to the president, her true influence on her husband may have been more abstract. Grant's aide Adam Badeau put it this way:

> *No one who did not know him intimately can ever say how much Mrs. Grant helped him; how she comforted him, and enabled him to perform his task, which, without that help and solace, I sometimes thought might never have been performed....She soothed him when cares oppressed him, she supported him when even he was downcast; she served him and nerved him at times when he needed all she did for him.*

Julia was the first president's wife to be the subject of a congressional inquiry. In an example of Julia's naivete or sense of entitlement, she accepted gifts, including using a yacht from Jay Gould and Jim Fisk. The men planned to purchase gold to drive up the price and invited Grant's brother-in-law Abel Corbin (married to his sister) to partner with them. Corbin's task was to write to Grant not to take action if gold prices seemed unstable. Grant didn't respond. Instead, he had Julia write to his sister and tell her, "My husband is annoyed by your husband's speculations. You must close them...quickly." Corbin warned his partners to abandon the plan, but not before Grant released gold reserves that stopped it. Still, the price of gold decreased and ruined many people. The inquiry absolved Julia and the president of wrongdoing in the investigation.

Criticisms

Julia did meet with criticism during her tenure.

For example, some said Julia and Ulysses were too permissive with their children. Their daughter was allowed to stay out late and drop out from a formal education. Even permitting the older ones to travel overseas was viewed as too permissive. And they allowed Nellie to marry an Englishman.

Julia was called out for her dress and appearance. She displayed too much neck and shoulder, and she dressed too matronly. Several times during her public life, Julia became concerned about her personal appearance because of her strabismus, beginning as early as the Civil War when photos of her, usually but not always in profile, circulated among the public. When she was a child, the family doctor said an operation could fix her eyes, but Julia refused. She rethought her decision as she grew older and was increasingly in the public eye. There are varying accounts of her attempt to have the operation as an adult. One claims the surgeon was ready to operate in a room in the White House when Ulysses found out and stopped it. But in her *Memoirs*, Julia gives the following account, which underscores Ulysses's love for his wife:

> *So I consulted the Doctor on this, to me, most delicate subject, but Alas! He told me it was too late, too late. I told the General and expressed my regret. He replied, "What in the world put such a thought in your head, Julia?" I said, "Why you are getting to be such a great man, and I am such a plain little wife. I thought if my eyes were as others are, I might not be so very, very plain…" He drew me to him and said, "Did I not fall in love with you with these same eyes? I like them just as they are, and now, remember, you are not to interfere with them. They are mine, and let me tell you, Mrs. Grant, you had better not make any experiments, as I might not like you half so well with any other eyes."*

Julia's response? "And I never did, my knight, my Lancelot."

Despite his popularity, Ulysses's two terms as president were tumultuous. There were triumphs—he and Secretary of State Fish settled bitterly contested claims against Great Britain arising from its support for Confederate raiders. He ordered the enforcement of new civil rights laws protecting African Americans that helped break the terror wreaked by the Ku Klux Klan in the conquered South. But his last term ended in multiple scandals, damaging his reputation for decades.

Perhaps the worst was the so-called Whiskey Ring affair, which involved corruption reaching into the White House. One of those implicated in a vast conspiracy to evade liquor taxes was Orville Babcock, Ulysses's former staff officer, presidential secretary and close friend. When the indictment was brought to him, Ulysses wrote on the back, "Let no guilty man escape if it can be avoided. Be especially vigilant…against all who insinuate that they have high influence to protect, or to protect them. No personal consideration should stand in the way of performing a public duty." Ulysses insisted on giving a deposition supporting Babcock's integrity. Babcock was acquitted but left the White House in favor of Ulysses's son Buck.

No Third Term

When the second term of Ulysses's presidency was winding down, Julia urged him to seek an unprecedented third term. Ulysses refused, but he made sure to tell the press before he told Julia because he knew it would make her unhappy.

Julia enjoyed living in the White House and was reluctant to leave it. The incoming president's wife, Lucy Hayes, invited her to ride to the inauguration ceremony with her, but Julia refused. After all, she'd already been to two. She stayed at the White House and prepared lunch for the Hayeses, even though she was no longer the sitting president's wife.

The only leave-taking sadder for Julia than that of quitting the White House was leaving White Haven for Ulysses's first posting after their marriage.

14

JULIA AFTER ULYSSES

What would the former president do after eight years in the White House? Ulysses and Julia decided to tour the world. They left the United States in May 1877 and returned in September 1879. Journalist John Russell Young covered the trip and gave a true sense of Julia in his chronicle of the journey. Public affection for her grew and continued, partly due to his depiction of her, for the rest of her life.

One story of Julia during the tour seemed particularly "Julia." In a visit to Queen Victoria, the queen spoke of being weary of all the official duties she had to perform. Julia, who seemed to disregard the fact Victoria reigned her country in her own right, said, "Yes, I can imagine them. I, too, have been the wife of a great ruler."

Upon their return to the United States, the Grants continued with a tour of the West before returning to their home in the East. They made a detour to Fort Vancouver, where Ulysses showed her the lonely post he served at in 1853. Huge crowds greeted them in Portland. Ulysses turned to his wife and said, "Julia, look there, see those people. This turn-out must be on your account, because when I came here before there were not three people on the dock."

In Leadville, Colorado, Julia donned the garb of a miner and descended into the mines. She did so simply to keep Ulysses from winning a secret bet he'd made with other men accompanying them that Julia would not go into the mine. Curiously, they bypassed Missouri on their way home.

WHITE HAVEN IS LOST

The Grants were "home," meaning they were in the United States, but they had no money—only property. There was no pension for former presidents, so there was nothing to look forward to in that area. A group of friends bought them a house in New York City, a grand home perfect for entertaining, and Julia used it to do so.

Grant permitted his son Buck to use his name in a Wall Street firm, which resulted in an income for the family that exceeded any they'd ever had. However, Julia mistrusted Buck's partner, Ferdinand Ward. Ward was known as the "Napoleon of Finance," but in the spring of 1884, the Grants, father and son, lost virtually everything to a Ponzi scheme established by Ward in the name of the partnership. (Ward was renamed the "Best Hated Man in the United States.")

William H. Vanderbilt loaned Ulysses $150,000, but it wasn't all charity. He took a mortgage on White Haven, and when the Grants couldn't pay the debt, he sold it at a foreclosure sale. Julia insisted they turn over all their property held in both names and gifts they'd received from world leaders on their tour to repay the debt. Limiting it to property in both names was a wise move on Julia's part. The New York house and the Grants' summer home in Long Branch, New Jersey, was in her name alone.

Vanderbilt refused the property and returned the gifts to Julia and Ulysses with the proviso that they donate them to the government in the name of the people. Grant insisted his friend keep the properties until Vanderbilt said he'd take the money from their sale and put it in trust for Julia. Ulysses was already worried about what would happen to her after he was gone. Grant agreed to this proposal, but Julia refused.

Julia immediately donated all their Civil War memorabilia and state gifts to the Smithsonian and signed over all their properties in Chicago, Washington and Philadelphia. The most difficult loss of "the dear old homestead in Missouri, White Haven." Julia said in her *Memoirs*, "[It] well-nigh broke my heart. My tears fell thick and fast; I could not help it." The Grants' last physical ties to St. Louis were gone.

ULYSSES'S LAST DAYS

The year 1884 saw a financial disaster for Ulysses and the beginning of a health crisis. He noticed a pain in his throat that doctors ultimately diagnosed as terminal throat cancer. He needed to do something to secure his family's future.

Samuel Clemens—better known to the American public as Mark Twain—first met Ulysses at a White House function in 1866. He was an admirer of the man who led the Union to victory. Nearly twenty years later, he and the general renewed their acquaintance. Several people urged Ulysses to write an autobiography and tell the world about this man, the son of a tanner, who led thousands and became president.

Clemens said that Ulysses had "no confidence in his ability to write well." Indeed, Ulysses told his doctor just a few days before his death, "If anyone had suggested the idea of becoming an author, as they frequently did, I was not sure whether they were making sport of me or not."

Clemens signed Ulysses to a very favorable contract. Ulysses completed his two-volume *Personal Memoirs* on July 19, 1885—eleven months after he first put pencil to paper. He died on July 23, 1885.

The work was an immediate bestseller. The royalties from the book—totaling $450,000 in nineteenth-century dollars (equivalent to $14 million today)—provided Julia with a comfortable living for the rest of her life. His *Personal Memoirs* are renowned as a work of art, not just personal history. Literary critic Edmund Wilson praised the writing as "perfect in concision and clearness, in its propriety and purity of language. Every word that Grant wrote has its purpose, yet everything seems understated." Ulysses's *Personal Memoirs* were first published on December 10, 1885, and have never gone out of print.

Julia spent all her time with Ulysses in his final days, always close to him. She prayed and held tight to the belief that as long as the cancer didn't progress, there was hope. It was empty hope in Ulysses's case. She told him jokes and tried to stay lighthearted.

When he died, her grief was so deep that she didn't attend his public funeral in New York.

Even after her husband died, his memory was still her main objective—his positive memory. After his death, Julia always referred to Ulysses as "the General," not "the President." She was most proud of his military accomplishments. She attended public events honoring her husband and traveled often to visit her children, three of whom lived in California.

Ida Dent, unidentified woman, Julia and Fred. After Ulysses died, Julia often appeared at events in his honor. This photo dates to the early 1900s and was probably taken at such an event. *Library of Congress.*

Julia was the first first lady to write her *Memoirs*, but she could find no one to publish them during her lifetime. Reasons vary. She wanted a deal equal to her husband's for his book, but no one was willing to offer that. Another theory, according to Nicholas Sacco from the U.S. Grant National Historic Site, is that she revealed too much personal information. Days were different then, and people didn't tell all. The *Memoirs* languished within the family until 1976 when Southern Illinois University Press in Carbondale, Illinois, published them. This volume relies heavily on Julia's work to tell her story. In fact, much of what we know about her comes from her *Memoirs*.

Julia died on December 14, 1902, in her Washington home. She remains beside Ulysses in death in Grant's Tomb in New York City.

Because of her openness to the press and public, her national exposure and her travel experiences, Julia Dent Grant died not a St. Louisan, not a Missourian, not a Westerner, but a national figure.

EPILOGUE

The family never regained White Haven after 1885. The farm fell into private hands. Most of the estate has been subdivided into lots with single-family homes. A large part south of Gravois Creek is now Grant's Farm, a family amusement venue and animal park, formerly the home of the Busch family. The main house was acquired by St. Louis County in 1986 and transferred to the National Park Service in 1989. The

White Haven as it appears today. The National Park Service decided to paint the house Paris green after uncovering a part of the original exterior during restoration. The Grants ordered it painted this popular Victorian color in 1874. *National Park Service.*

Hardscrabble today on Grant's Farm. *Vicki Berger Erwin.*

Ulysses S. Grant National Historic Site has only about ten acres of the original estate. Visitors can tour the home as it was when Ulysses and Julia owned it after the Civil War, with the addition of an inside kitchen and Paris Green—a popular color of the Victorian era—exterior paint.

Even though the Grants lived in Hardscrabble for only three months, there has been a unique fascination with the log cabin for more than one hundred years. Luther Conn sold the cabin to Edwin and Justin Joy, two real estate developers. They disassembled the structure, numbering each log, and reassembled it in the Old Orchard area of Webster Groves, Missouri, a suburb of St. Louis. C.F. Blanke bought the cabin in 1903 and moved it next to the building now known as the St. Louis Art Museum for display during the St. Louis World's Fair in 1904 as an advertisement for his company's coffee. In 1907, August Busch Sr. bought the cabin and moved it to Grant's Farm, where it can be seen today when touring the farm, as well as from Gravois Road. The Daughters of the American Revolution placed a monument in St. Paul's Cemetery on the original site of Hardscrabble.

BIBLIOGRAPHY

Berkin, Carol. *Civil War Wives*. Alfred A. Knopf, 2009.

Broughton, Samuel C. “Revelations of Soldier’s Life.” Marion County MOGenWeb. https://momarion.genealogyvillage.com.

Carlin, Diana B. “Julia Dent Grant: A General’s Wife in the White House.” Ulysses S. Grant Historic Site, January 28, 2024. https://www.nps.gov/ulsg/index.htm.

———. “Ulysses S. Grant as Julia Saw Him.” U.S. Grant Symposium, July 26, 2024.

Carlin, Diana B., Anita B. McBride and Nancy Kegan Smith. *Remember the First Ladies*. Cognella Press, 2024.

Casey, Emma Dent. “When Grant Went A-Courtin.” Ulysses S. Grant National Historic Site, https://www.nps.gov/ulsg/index.htm.

Chernow, Ron. *My Dearest Julia: The Wartime Letters of Ulysses S. Grant to His Wife*. Library of America, 2018.

Clarke, Frances M., and Rebecca J. Plant. “‘The Most Woebegone Twelve-Year-Old Lad in America’: Frederick Dent Grant’s Civil War.” *Emerging Civil War*, February 3, 2023. https://emergingcivilwar.com.

College of St. Scholastica. Ulysses S. Grant Information Center. https://libguides.css.edu/usgrant/home.

Cox, Kim C., ed. *Colonel Grant’s Regiment: The 21st Illinois Volunteers from Muster to Stones River in the Letters for Private Allen M. Patton*. Privately printed, 1997.

Daily Missouri Republican. “The Early Life of Gen. Grant by His Father.” March 15, 1868.

. “Trustee Sale.” August 21, 1860.

Danisi, Thomas C., and Raymond W. Wood. "Lewis and Clark's Route Map: James MacKay's Map of the Missouri River." *Western Historical Quarterly* 35, no. 1 (Spring 2004): 53–72.

First Ladies Library. "Julia Dent Grant Biography." http://archive.firstladies.org.

Garland, Hamlin. *Ulysses S. Grant: His Life and Character*. Doubleday & McClure, 1898.

Grant, Jesse R. *In the Day of My Father General Grant*. Harper and Brothers Publishing, 1925.

Grant, J.R. "The Early Life of Gen. Grant By His Father." *Ulysses S. Grant Association Newsletter* 8, no. 2 (January 1971)

———. "Grant as Remembered by His Father." *Ulysses S. Grant Association Newsletter* 8, no. 1 (October 1970).

Grant, Julia Dent. *The Personal Memoirs of Julia Dent Grant.* 45th anniversary edition. Southern Illinois University Press, 2020.

Grant, Ulysses S. *The Annotated Memoirs of Ulysses S. Grant*. Edited by Elizabeth D. Samet. Liveright Publishing, 2019.

———. *The Papers of Ulysses S. Grant*. 32 vols. Edited by John Y. Simon and John Marsalek. Southern Illinois Press, 1967–2013.

Hooper, Candice Shy. *Lincoln's Generals' Wives*. Kent State University Press, 2016.

———. "The Two Julias." *New York Times*, February 14, 2013.

Lee, Olive. "The Women of the Grant Family." *New England Magazine*, series 20, no. 4, 1903–04.

Lewis, Lloyd. *Captain Sam Grant*. Little, Brown, 1950.

Little, Kimberly Scott. *Ulysses S. Grant's White Haven: A Place Where Extraordinary People Came to Live Extraordinary Lives*. National Park Service, 1993.

National Park Service. *Cultural Landscape Report.* Ulysses S. Grant National Historic Site, 2024.

———. "Ellen Wrenshall Dent." Ulysses S. Grant National Historic Site. https://www.nps.gov.

———. "Frederick F. Dent." Ulysses S. Grant National Historic Site. https://www.nps.gov.

———. "Jule." Ulysses S. Grant National Historic Site. www.nps.gov.

———. "Whitehaven: The Original Dent Family Home in Maryland." Ulysses S. Grant National Historic Site. https://www.nps.gov.

Oakley, E.M. "Psychic First Lady." *Psychic Magazine* 9, no. 4 (1976).

O'Bright, Alan W. *The Farm on the Gravois: Historic Structure Report*. Ulysses S. Grant National Historic Site, 1999.

O'Neil, Tim. "Ulysses Grant's Marriage Here Was a Quiet Affair." *St. Louis Post-Dispatch*, August 24, 2022. https://www.stltoday.com.

Perry, Mark. *Grant and Twain: The Story of an American Friendship*. Random House, 2005.

Post, James L., comp. *Reminiscences by Personal Friends of Gen. U.S. Grant and the History of Grant's Log Cabin*. J.L. Post, 1904.

Reeves, John. *Soldier of Destiny: Slavery, Secession, and the Redemption of Ulysses S. Grant*. Pegasus Books, 2023.

Ross, Ishbell. *The General's Wife*. Arcadia Press, 2019.

Rosza, Matthew. "The True Story of the President Who Couldn't Hear Music." *Salon*, December 12, 2022. https://www.salon.com.

Sacco, Nicholas W. "All in the Family: Ulysses and Julia Grant's Relationship with Their In-Laws." In *Grant at 200: Reconsidering the Life and Legacy of Ulysses S. Grant*, edited by Chris Mackowski and Frank J. Scaturro. Savis Beatie, 2023.

———. "'I Never Was an Abolitionist': Ulysses S. Grant and Slavery, 1854–1863." *Journal of the Civil War Era* 9, no. 3 (September 2019): 410–37.

———. "The Mystery of William Jones, An Enslaved Man Owned by Ulysses S. Grant." *Journal of the Civil War Era*, December 7, 2018. https://www.journalofthecivilwarera.org.

Shields, Clara McGeorge. "General Grant at Fort Humboldt in the Early Days." *Ulysses S. Grant Association Newsletter* 8, no. 3 (April 1971).

Songer, Abram. "Civil War Story." Private collection of Curt Wittbracht (used with permission).

Stevens, Walter B. *Grant in St. Louis*. Applewood Books, n.d.

Teeters, Kristopher. *Practical Liberators: Union Officers in the Western Theater During the Civil War*. University of North Carolina Press, 2018.

Ulysses S. Grant and Julia B. Grant v. Joseph W. White. Missouri Supreme Court, No. 1137 (February Term 1866), Box 62, Folder 18, *Missouri Judicial Records Database*. https://s1.sos.mo.gov.

———. 43 Mo. 285 (Mo. 1868).

White, Ronald C. *American Ulysses: A Life of Ulysses S. Grant*. Random House, 2016.

Wilson, Edmund. *Patriotic Gore*. Farrar, Strauss, Giroux, 1961.

Wolk, Greg. "Ulysses Grant in Northern Missouri, July 1861." *Emerging Civil War*, August 16, 2024. https://emergingcivilwar.com.

ABOUT THE AUTHORS

Vicki Berger Erwin has worked in the publishing industry for more than thirty years in various capacities, including sales, book distribution and as the owner of a bookstore in St. Charles, Missouri. She is the author of more than thirty books in varied genres: picture books, middle-grade novels, local histories and true crime.

James W. Erwin practiced law in St. Louis for thirty-seven years. He is the author of seven books on local history.

This is their fourth book together. They live in Crestwood, Missouri, not far from the Ulysses S. Grant National Historic Site, along with their dog Luna, who enjoys walking on the grounds of White Haven.